I0568967

THE MAGNITUDE OF GOD

EXPLORING THE DIVINE

BRIAN POE

CYPRESS

Copyright © 2022 by Brian Poe

The Magnitude of God: Exploring the Divine

Manufactured in the United States of America

Cataloging-in-Publication Data

Poe, Brian, 1982-

The magnitude of God: exploring the divine / Brian Poe

p. cm.

ISBN 978-1-956811-35-3 (paperback) 978-1-956811-36-0 (ebook)

Library of Congress Control Number: 2022918763

1. God (Christianity)–Attributes I. Author. II. Title.

231.1—dc20

Cover design by Brad McKinnon and Brittany Vander Maas.

Pronouns referring to Deity are capitalized except when quoting from the New International Version (NIV).

All rights reserved.

No part of this book may be reproduced in any form or by any electronic or mechanical means, including information storage and retrieval systems, without written permission from the author, except for the use of brief quotations in a book review.

Cypress Publications
3625 Helton Drive
PO Box HCU
Florence, AL 35630

www.hcu.edu/publications

To my loving wife, Jesse, and also to my boys, Caleb and Benjamin, who have suffered patiently with me through the many hours taken to write this book. They have endured the journey with me in love.

CONTENTS

BIBLE ABBREVIATIONS

Old Testament

Gen	Genesis
Exod	Exodus
Lev	Leviticus
Num	Numbers
Deut	Deuteronomy
Josh	Joshua
Judg	Judges
Ruth	Ruth
1–2 Sam	1–2 Samuel
1–2 Kgs	1–2 Kings
1–2 Chr	1–2 Chronicles
Ezra	Ezra
Neh	Nehemiah
Esth	Esther
Job	Job
Ps	Psalms
Prov	Proverbs
Eccl	Ecclesiastes

Song	Song of Solomon
Isa	Isaiah
Jer	Jeremiah
Lam	Lamentations
Ezek	Ezekiel
Dan	Daniel
Hos	Hosea
Joel	Joel
Amos	Amos
Obad	Obadiah
Jonah	Jonah
Mic	Micah
Nah	Nahum
Hab	Habakkuk
Zeph	Zephaniah
Hag	Haggai
Zech	Zechariah
Mal	Malachi

New Testament

Matt	Matthew
Mark	Mark
Luke	Luke
John	John
Acts	Acts
Rom	Romans
1–2 Cor	1–2 Corinthians
Gal	Galatians
Eph	Ephesians
Phil	Philippians
Col	Colossians
1–2 Thess	1–2 Thessalonians
1–2 Tim	1–2 Timothy
Titus	Titus
Phlm	Philemon
Heb	Hebrews
Jas	James
1–2 Pet	1–2 Peter
1–2–3 John	1–2–3 John
Jude	Jude
Rev	Revelation

INTRODUCTION

Lord, our Lord,
how majestic is your name in all the earth!
You have set your glory
in the heavens.

The God I am going to write about in this book is real. However, the stories are ancient and may seem foreign; nevertheless, they are real. Because the distance of time, the stories of God can sometimes lose their sense of reality and connection to humanity. The fear, the dignity, the power, the majesty and awe grow faint. Humanity increasingly seems left here on this planet godless. This book has one purpose; I want to remind the reader of the greatness of God. What it will do to you may be vastly different than its impact on me; nonetheless, I believe a fresh knowledge of God will change lives.

The power of God has been demonstrated in these past two millennia differently than it was during the two testaments. I believe God is still full of power, but let's face it, He does not reveal Himself in a cloud of fire as He once did. I have not seen waters part since the time of Elijah and Elisha. I read through the Old Testament and I see a God who is evident in and through creation; but today, I look out the window and I see rain clouds and a muddy driveway. Things seem to be different than it was even in the New Testament Scriptures. I understand and am aware that there are countless and a wide variety of theologies explaining the power of God today. Yet what seems to be unmistakable is that things are different. I read through the New Testament and see people being healed just by the shadow of Peter falling upon them. Paul and Silas sang while in prison, and with an earthquake the prison crumbled; through such a demonstration of power, many were saved that night. One day while Jesus was preaching, they could not get to Him, so they lowered a lame man through the roof; Jesus tells him to rise and he stands to his feet. Things are not as they used to be from what I can tell. Got is still powerful, but His power is demonstrated differently than it was. Through this book, I hope to demonstrate that.

This is my understanding of how to grapple with this change: we live in a very unspiritual culture, especially in the Western American culture. Why? because we don't see the physical demonstrative evidence of God in our lives. Because of this, it is easy to allow God, His voice, His handiwork, His reverence, and His fear all fade into the background. We—*I*, as a by-product, sometimes forget who I worship as I ought to; sometimes I stop worshipping Him. Because I have at times forgotten the majesty of His great voice, I have forgotten the power and His reverence. Because of this, I do not fear as I ought to. At the end of the day, I sometimes do not worship in awe as God deserves.

This book is my journey to coming to understand God in

a way that He is. Even though I do not see God in the same way He once demonstrated, I want to know Him the same and with the same reverence. My goal is to better know God as one who deserves worship and reverence. Furthermore, I want to unveil God as I see Him in Scripture. I hope to unveil his personality and characteristics that perhaps some have forgotten. We are going to look at the voice of God and the ways it shook the earth in power. We are going to look at the presence of God that the earth could not even contain. We are going to look at the testimonies of those who spoke of God, including those who were not of Israel. Finally, we are going to take time to look at the reverence of God and His great power through different stories in Scripture.

David walked out on his rooftop one night and looked up into the sky and considered the stars; his conclusion was simple: "Lord, our Lord, how majestic is your name in all the earth! You have set your glory in the heavens" (Ps 8:2). That is what I want to come back to; that is what I want all of us to come back to. And I also understand from Scripture that God has never changed (Mal 3:6). I am the one who needs to change and return to a real and appropriate understanding of God. Through this work, I hope that you begin to see God for who He is. I hope you see the greatness of God and realize that He is still great and has amazing things in store for you. I hope that you will understand the power of the Almighty, so when He says he wants to continue the work He started in you, that will excite you and you will be in wonder of what the powerful hand of God can do if allowed to form the rough edges of your heart. The journey begins right now. If you dare see the Almighty in ways you may never have, turn the page.

PART 1: THE VOICE OF GOD

Speak to us yourself and we will listen. But do not have God speak to us or we will die.

—Children of Israel

Moses was on Mount Sinai for many days receiving the law from God. The people saw thunder and lightning, the mountain shook and it was covered with smoke. It was during this time that the people were learning who God was. The children of Israel, also called Hebrews or Israelites, were enslaved in Egypt for many generations. The only thing handed down about God and ethics would have been stories. It was likely they were void of being allowed to enjoy most practices of worship or offerings to their God. For several hundred years, they would have been submersed in the ideas of Egyptian culture, rather than that of their forefathers. The knowledge of the true God was known, but for some, it was becoming a blur of folklore.

The Hebrews received a wake-up call when Moses came

to deliver them. We do not have the content of the stories they were saying to each other in their homes, but I am sure their dinner conversations were full of surprise and amazement. Every day they would watch Moses come, talk to Pharaoh, and call down a plague. Things were changing. Life was changing. They were beginning to know their God in a new way.

After watching the terrifying plagues, the children of Israel were again dumbfounded as they watched the waters of the Red Sea part and they were able to walk on dry ground. I can only imagine the awe as they walked through. How do you just walk through a sea without curiosity and wonder flooding your mind? A few more days pass by, their journey continues and they come to Mount Sinai. The same God who performed the ten phenomenal plagues was up on the mountain talking with Moses. The same God who parted the waters of a sea was causing the mountain to tremble. The past few weeks for the Hebrews were a crash course on the knowledge of God. All their stories were coming to life right before their eyes. Yet, their stories did not give God justice; their stories did not speak of plagues, water parting, or such power so mighty to shake a mountain. They heard that He was the Creator and divided the waters in the beginning, but that reality began to take new form as they saw the waters of the Red Sea part right before their eyes. Who is this God?

The children of Israel were standing at the base of the mountain. Moses, who had been up on the mountain with God for a few days, came down to speak to them. Their response was quite telling:

> When the people saw the thunder and lightning and heard the trumpet and saw the mountain in smoke, they trembled with fear. They stayed at a distance and said to Moses,

"Speak to us yourself and we will listen. But do not have God speak to us or we will die" (Exod 20:18–19 NIV).

They were fearful with good reason; they were getting a glimpse of the Almighty, and it was quite a remarkable knowledge to lay hold of. But what they were not aware of is that God was pursuing His people. God wanted to know them, and for them to know Him—He wanted a covenant with them. If they would only learn His voice.

One's voice tells us much about a person. The way people use their voices, the tone, the volume, and how much they talk—all are tales to who a person is. The Israelites knew God was powerful; they watched Him perform the plagues and part the waters, but they did not *know* Him yet, and they were far from a full surrender of faith. Only a few days after arriving at Mount Sinai, they would build a golden calf. Why? because they thought God had killed Moses on the mountain. Their first response was to build a calf to worship instead. That is not a response of one who knows God—they had no clue.

In that moment, standing before Moses who came down to speak with them, the people did not want to hear the voice of God. Perhaps they were fearful of the powerful God they were learning so much about so fast. Perhaps they were fearful of what they knew was in their hearts; idolatry and other Egyptian practices. I would propose that both were true. They were afraid of what they knew and also afraid of knowing more. Furthermore, they are afraid of being known.

God wanted them to hear His voice. Notice, when they first arrived at Mount Sinai, God spoke to Moses, but He wanted to do so where the people could hear; "I am going to come to you in a dense cloud, so that the people will hear me speaking with you and will always put their trust in you" (Exod 19:9). Even after all that they had seen, there was something about hearing the voice of God that seemed important to God. I believe God knew He had adequately revealed how powerful He was, but He wanted their knowledge of Him to be deeper and more personal—He wanted them to know His voice. He wanted them to hear Him speak to their leader; the love, the concern, the direction—He wanted them to *know* that they were His people, and He wanted to be their God.

A few days later, the mountain was still trembling and was smoke covered. Moses tried to bridge the gap between God and the people; "Then Moses led the people out of the camp to meet with God, and they stood at the foot of the mountain" (Exod 19:17). The Israelites would have been accustomed to pagan gods who were distant from their people. But now they were being drawn by the God of Abraham in a way they never perceived. They had been invited into a covenant with the Creator. As soon as they came to Mount Sinai, just days after the Red Sea, God told Moses to tell the people the following:

> You yourselves have seen what I did to Egypt, and how I carried you on eagles' wings and brought you to myself. Now if you obey me fully and keep my covenant, then out of all nations you will be my treasured possession. Although the whole earth is mine, you will be for me a kingdom of priests and a holy nation (Exod 19:4–6).

This is a lot to take in. Disbelief would have flooded their thoughts—an enemy hard to defeat. Fear would have made them skeptical. The invitation had been given.

But the people did not want to hear the voice of God. It

would deepen their knowledge of Him. It would reveal His love and mercy. But they let fear hold them back from this incredible moment. The same fear that would keep them out of the Promised Land two years later. Because of fear, they wanted rather to be distant from God and feel safe than be close to Him. God wanted them to know who He really was.

The voice of God is revealing of His character, His nature, and His essence. The very purpose of the opening part of this book is that we can see God in the way He wanted men and women to see Him from long ago. As early as the garden, there has been a special place for hearing the voice of God. In this first part, we will examine stories where the voice of God was uttered. What was the tone of that voice? Did mountains tremble, or was it as soft as a whisper? What did He say and what does that speak about God's character?

When you read through these chapters, listen to His voice and learn about your God. But listen carefully—sometimes His voice can be so powerful to disrupt the elements of nature, while other times, it might only be heard in a gentle breeze. One thing is for certain, His voice is life-changing.

1

THE VOICE THAT CREATES

In the beginning God created the heavens and the earth. Now the earth was formless and empty, darkness was over the surface of the deep, and the Spirit of God was hovering over the waters (Gen 1:1–2).

The Word of God had to begin with a phrase, a sentence of some sort. The narrative of the first four-thousand years had to begin with a statement that was worthy of all the following days and events to fit under. The beginning words of any letter or document are the most difficult. Was Moses the writer of Genesis? Therein is much debate, but for the intent of this chapter, it does not matter. The writer of Genesis sits down, takes a pen, rests it on the scroll, and he moves the pen that would etch words not only onto the parchment, but into eternity. The words penned would steer the course of every theological idea since conceived. Trying to find the words that would begin life, words that would inaugurate the creation narrative and would begin our pursuit of knowing God, the writer sits and ponders. There was only one beginning, and there has always been only one God. And during this beginning, there was *only* God. Finally, the words come:

In the beginning God...

In hindsight, I don't think there are four English words that could better begin such a story. There was a moment at the beginning where there was only One—and He was God. And there was a moment when the universe, in its fullness and yet its emptiness, stood still—the moment when God spoke:

And God said, "Let there be light," and there was light. God saw that the light was good, and he separated the light from the darkness. God called the light "day," and the darkness he called "night." And there was evening, and there was morning—the first day.

And God said, "Let there be a vault between the waters to separate water from water." So God made the vault and separated the water under the vault from the water above it. And it was so. God called the vault "sky." And there was evening, and there was morning—the second day.

And God said, "Let the water under the sky be gathered to one place, and let dry ground appear." And it was so. God called the dry ground "land," and the gathered waters he called "seas." And God saw that it was good.

Then God said, "Let the land produce vegetation: seed-bearing plants and trees on the land that bear fruit with seed in it, according to their various kinds." And it was so. The land produced vegetation: plants bearing seed according to their kinds and trees bearing fruit with seed in it according to their kinds. And God saw that it was good. And there was evening, and there was morning—the third day.

And God said, "Let there be lights in the vault of the sky to separate the day from the night, and let them serve as signs to mark sacred times, and days and years, and let them be lights in the vault of the sky to give light on the earth." And it was so. God made two great lights—the greater light to govern the day and the lesser light to govern the night. He also made the stars. God set them in the vault of the sky to give light on the earth, to govern the day and the night, and to separate light from darkness. And God saw that it was good. And there was evening, and there was morning—the fourth day.

And God said, "Let the water teem with living creatures, and let birds fly above the earth across the vault of the sky." So God created the great creatures of the sea and every living thing with which the water teems and that moves about in it, according to their kinds, and every winged bird according to its kind. And God saw that it was good. God blessed them and said, "Be fruitful and increase in number and fill the water in the seas, and let the birds increase on the earth." And there was evening, and there was morning—the fifth day.

And God said, "Let the land produce living creatures according to their kinds: the livestock, the creatures that move along the ground, and the wild animals, each according to its kind." And it was so. God made the wild animals according to their kinds, the livestock according to their kinds, and all the creatures that move along the

ground according to their kind. And God saw that it was
good.

Then God said, "Let us make man in our image, in our like-
ness, so that they may rule over the fish in the sea and the
birds in the sky, over the livestock and all the wild animals,
and over all the creatures that move along the ground."
    … God saw all that he had made, and it was good. (Gen
1:3–26, 31a)

Our attention is going to be directed toward one
powerful feature of God, and in fact, the only thing we have
from Him in this beginning chapter—His voice. In the beginning, there was only God, and He created all that is from
nothing. The very next word from the statement that began
it all tells us that in the beginning God *created*. Many things
have been created by man. Sometimes we use our hands,
sometimes we use machinery, but God used neither. The
creating force of God that turned nothing into a vast
universe was *His voice*. Standing in the midst of all the noth-
ingness that had yet to be created, God alone began to create.
In His presence was no matter to create with; He created all
that is from nothing. With a voice unimaginable and power
therein that cannot be contained, God spoke.

I think we take for granted this event, and perhaps we
downplay it a great deal. Most of us have been told this story
from a very early age by our parents or in Sunday school.
However, because of that and other factors, I believe we have
forgotten the magnitude of such an event. Furthermore,
when we speak of the creation story, we usual go through the
seven days as they are detailed in the narrative. There is
nothing wrong with this, but we often neglect to see,
standing there alone just moments before anything existed,

our God. Furthermore, we often neglect to take notice of that moment when the only noise heard was His voice. There was no traffic, no sound of birds, not even the rushing of the wind or water. There was silence in the emptiness— and when all was silent, God uttered His voice into the cosmos.

What did the voice of God sound like? I can envision the world taking form and matter coming into existence; it is a reach for my imagination, but I can see it. But what I cannot fully grasp is the sound of His voice. Besides the evident fact that He is our Creator, this is the earliest that we begin to *know* our God. They say a baby can hear his/her parents' voice from within the womb, and right away a bonding begins—a relationship begins. This is the earliest we get to hear the voice of our Creator. This is the moment we get the first glimpse of our God. When we hear His voice, if we are not distracted by the worlds forming, when we listen closely, we will know Him more.

I am almost lost for words as I am trying to understand that moment in time. I stay quiet and listen as I imagine what that moment sounded like when God first spoke everything into existence, but nothing in my imagination seems to fit. My first inclination is that His voice was loud and thunder-ous. And when the first words were spoken, every existing atom shook vigorously as it was commanded to become something good. After all, we equate volume and depth with power. But God had no need to prove to anyone His power; He was not trying to make a point as we see in later cases such as Job. Perhaps His voice was soft and confident. Many might recall movies where the bad guy speaks with a soft tone and confidence. A voice that needs not to prove anything, nor is it in need for volume to enhance the force of its command. So, perhaps it was in a gentle voice that God spoke; gentle, but containing the unfathomable power to create worlds. A gentle command that did not need anything but to be spoken. We do not know the tone or volume God spoke with during those seven days, but we know there was power therein.

What people do with their power speaks much of their character. In history, we have seen some use power to destroy and do evil. We have seen others hold onto power, yet do nothing with it. And of course, there have been those who used power to do good. What do we learn about God with His use of power? The first thing we learn about God is His desire for relationships. With all power at His disposal and with a desire to be connected, He creates humanity. I think we forget about this when listening to what David and Jeremiah said about being known by God yet in the womb (Ps 139:15–16; Jer 1:5). Or when Jesus said that even the hairs on our head are numbered by God (Luke 12:7). We are not merely created creatures. We are created as *treasures* whom God loves, and He loves to know us and loves to be known. When we imagine this truth about God, it is unbelievably humbling; a God of such power and majesty created each of us to know us. We can let that sink in, but I don't think it will ever sink far enough to fully grasp it.

Here is when the message becomes real: When God finished such a feat that has never been equaled, He came down to the garden and walked in the cool of the day desiring to walk and talk with Adam and Eve. As we journey through these pages, we will see a powerful God whose power none can contend. Yet, we will also see that the heart of the Almighty God is tender and full of compassion, and He loves his creation.

There is only one God. There was a day when He stood in the empty cosmos and spoke. No other sound was heard, for there was nothing else until He spoke, and after He spoke there was everything that is. There is good reason why early civilizations had a *big* image of God. He is and always has been so powerful that when He speaks, things change, lives are transformed, and worlds are created.

That is our God.

2

THE DAY GOD SPOKE TO JOB

I remember as a child sometimes I would do some foolish things and need a scolding—sometimes a spanking. Don't get me wrong, there were plenty of times my dad would talk gently and just tell me what I did wrong. But there were those times when he really needed to get the point through to my wayward mind. So, I would stand there as he would use that *dad* tone and would speak with a voice that in itself was sometimes terrifying. It was always tough standing there. I was afraid to move, and I wouldn't dare turn my head or look away from him. I would stand there and stare and give full attention. The world felt like it stopped spinning; time stood still. I want to be clear, however, I deserved it. In hindsight, I appreciate those times; they formed me into the man that I am. Many reading this may have had similar experiences. But don't be fooled, what I am going to show you in this chapter is far more intense. It is one thing when my dad got upset and had to scold me, it is quite another thing to have God thunder his voice. We are privileged with another moment in time that helps us to know who our God is. We are going to look at a time when God again spoke, revealing His greatness and power—revealing Himself. In the story of Job, we will realize this to be exactly God's intent—God wanted Job to remember and to know how great his God was.

Most of us know the story of Job, but do we recall what the book of Job tells us about God? This is a story about Job and the dialogue with him and his friends, but it also tells us about a God who laid the foundation of the world, who set the boundaries for the water, who gave the command to the sunset, who called forth the constellations in their seasons and tamed the beastly and unequaled leviathan. In my opinion, we learn more about God when He spoke to Job in these few chapters than we do in the rest of the Bible. Job was about to be awakened—Job was about to know his God in a way that he had never known before—Job was about to learn the unmeasurable greatness of God.

Job was a blessed man with a wonderful family and much wealth. The first chapter of Job says "he had seven sons and three daughters, and he owned seven thousand sheep, three thousand camels, five hundred yoke of oxen and five hundred donkeys ..." (Job 1:2–3). However, his life was upheaved when everything he had was taken from him in just a matter of a day. And it was not long later that he also got boils all over his body. The emotional and physical pain of what he had to go through was excruciating and nearly too much to bear. However, Job's friends came to comfort him and offer some advice. This was when things began to turn toward a peculiar end—an end that only God had in mind.

Their intentions were pure; they truly only wanted the best for Job, but Job's friends failed to see the big picture of what God was doing. Job's friends began to accuse him of harboring sin; after all, God would not bring such distress to a righteous person. They went back and forth with Job only for Job to contend that he was innocent.

Job's response to this immediate downfall in his life was a model to even the best of us. As the story began, we keep reading as we have no idea what to expect from Job. However, we read to Job 1:20 where it says Job fell on his face and worshipped. Job did not understand what was happening and had no clue why, but there he was with his life in ruins. Yet in all of that, he maintained his integrity. Job's friends responded in the most logical manner saying God would not allow such downfall to come upon a righteous man. To this point, Job did not disagree, but Job was perplexed because he did not know in what way he had sinned. The dialogue continued between Job and his friends while emotions were on the rise. The comforting console became a heated debate between Job and his friends. All the more, Job knew that with every fiber within himself, he did nothing to deserve what was happening. There was only one place left to cast the blame—on God.

After Job's friends repeatedly combat him to admit his sin, and after Job truly searched his heart attempting to find any sin to deserve such a plot, he found none. Consequently, Job began to question the justice of God. Justice is a paramount divine quality of God, but now it was being questioned by Job. Job replied to his friend Bildad saying, "Though I cry, 'Violence!' I get no response; though I call for help, there is no justice" (Job 19:7). This may not seem like an accusation toward God, but where else is Job expecting to find justice? None other than God. Later Job responds to all of his friends saying, "As surely as God lives, who has denied me justice, the Almighty, who has made my life bitter" (Job 27:2). Said simply, "God, this is your fault; I am in the right,

You are in the wrong." While questioning God's justice, Job spoke of his own justice while given his final defense: "I put on righteousness as my clothing; justice was my robe and my turban" (Job 29:14). It is not clear at first, but when you look closely, you see that Job had made firm claims to have maintained his own justice, while at the same time he began to question the justice of God. The Almighty had been silent through all of this, but He would soon speak in ways that would change everything—a storm was coming—God was coming.

On the horizon, a storm began to brew. Did God need to come in a storm? No, He did not, but it was most fitting for how He would speak to Job and the impression He wanted to give. Even though He would speak with a force and authority that would shake the heavens, God would also have the power of nature to demonstrate the magnitude of the moment. Job was about to be encountered by God in measures that would peak the capability of what Job could handle. And because of this, God told Job to brace himself like a man. Can you imagine such a moment as that? Imagine you are standing there and God comes to speak to you. But He tells you that you better hold on to whatever you can because things are going to get a little rough. Such a moment would simply be terrifying.

The powerful monologue of God spans from chapters thirty-eight to the end of forty-one (I encourage you to read these chapters before you continue). Due to the length, we will only look at small portions. God began to speak in the storm:

Then the Lord spoke to Job out of the storm. He said: "Who is this that obscures my plans with words without knowledge? Brace yourself like a man; I will question you, and you shall answer me. Where were you when I laid the earth's foundation? Tell me, if you understand. Who marked off its dimensions? Surely you know! Who stretched a measuring line across it? On what were its footings set, or who laid its cornerstone?" (Job 38:1–6)

God continued through the next two chapters with a forceful declaration of his power. Before this moment, while struggling through his trials, Job was beginning to have a small image of God as he thought he could blame God for injustice. God thought it necessary to remind Job of a few things. Just when it seemed like God might have been done and Job thought he was allowed to respond, God continued to speak:

The Lord said to Job: "Will the one who contends with the Almighty correct him? Let him who accuses God answer him!" Then Job answered the Lord: "I am unworthy—how can I repay you? I put my hand over my mouth. I spoke once, but I have no answer—twice, but I will say no more." Then the Lord spoke to Job out of the storm: "Brace yourself like a man; I will question you, and you shall answer me. Would you discredit my justice? Would you condemn me to justify yourself? Do you have an arm like God's, and can your voice thunder like this?" (Job 40:1–9)

Job got a few words in, but he was quickly interrupted as God continued again to explain to Job who He was. God did not want to be *repaid*, He wanted Job to understand the nature of His God. Continuing for another two chapters, God spoke of the mighty Behemoth which He said He not only made, but can approach it with a sword. He also spoke of the unequaled Leviathan which, though a fierce and terrifying predator, God simply said it was no match for Him. Job was beginning to understand.

After bracing himself and listening to the thunderous voice of God declaring His majestic qualities, Job understood. When God finished His speech, Job humbly responded to God:

> I know that you can do all things; no purpose of yours can be thwarted. You asked, "Who is this that obscures my plans without knowledge?" Surely I spoke of things I did not understand, things too wonderful for me to know. (Job 42:2–3)

Job finally understood God in a way that he had never before. Job finally understood that he did not fully understand. Furthermore, Job understood that the things that were happening were not out of evil intent done by an unjust God, but rather things that were *too wonderful* for him to understand. It came down to a matter of perception. Job came to understand that God was doing something good, although he did not know what it was.

What do we learn from God in these chapters? If we look closely, we will see much more than Job holding on to whatever he could grab to survive that terrifying moment. This story paints an intriguing image full of fascination, but there is more to see. If you look, some things are right up front while some are hiding in the background, nonetheless, we will see fascinating things about God.

One of the first things we see, as Job was meant to see, is that God is unparalleled in every aspect—He is Mighty! God first set the tone that He was the one that set the earth's foundations, *and Job was not there.* God also established that the waters obey His command and have stayed at the boundaries God had set. God told of the channels of water and the paths of storms, and how He created both. He spoke of how He set the constellations in their seasons. The moments God was speaking to Job were the purest revelation of the essence of God that anyone had the privilege to hear. God revealed His power and sovereignty over every creature and beast, every storm and drought. He not only commanded the stars, but He set them in place. When Job heard these words, he would have been humbly in awe having this fresh revelation of his God. He was not man that He could be accused. He was not equal to man. That day, by the time the storm was over, Job knew the unmatched magnitude of his God.

The second thing we learn about God during these chapters is that He takes pride in character—His justice. The justice of God is not a hidden attribute of God throughout the Bible. A person can find passages speaking of God's justice in nearly all sixty-six books. God intended for us to know that He is a just God, and on that day, in the storm, God wanted Job to know just that. We learned earlier that Job was implying that God was unjust with His dealing with him. We read God's response: "Would you discredit my justice? Would you condemn me to justify yourself" (Job 40:8)? God intended for Job to know that injustice was not in any measure a part of His nature; Job simply didn't understand. Furthermore, God wanted Job to know that a man cannot take up cause against God; our best course of action is to seek to understand. God wanted Job to know that he may not have understood what was going on, but God had remained *just* in every action. It is His nature—God was and always will be *just*.

One final thing we learn about God in these chapters is the desire God had to see Job grow and succeed. Having the text before us, we understand that the plan of God from the start was to bless Job. Of course, Job did not understand this, but God intended good things for him. Furthermore, we see that God did not want Job to fail. If you noticed, the reason God had to speak in these chapters was to realign Job's view of his God. Before this, what we see is a confused man who had no clue what was happening, and was close to missing it. In the early chapters, Job stood so strong, but when he began to question God's justice, he was setting himself up for failure. But out of the good nature of God, He was not about to let Job fail. God spoke to Job in the storm and Job was reminded of the wonderful qualities, and most of all, the justice of his God. At the end of the story, Job was blessed. I think what is important to see here is that this victory is to God's credit. Yes, Job was a great man, but on his own, he was headed toward failure. As it is for us even now, our victory and blessings are to God's credit.

I will never say this is all we learn about God in those chapters in Job; rather I will contend that those few chapters do not even come close to explaining the magnitude of our God. Perhaps you saw others aspects of God in those chapters that I did not. Let Him reveal Him to you. Let Him be your mighty God. He is not *as big as* those four chapters in Job; in those chapters, we only get a glimpse—God is so much bigger. I hope during the remainder of these pages, you will see a few more glimpses of your most wonderful and amazing God.

THE STILL VOICE

I learned something about God in my time studying His character and nature; I have learned that as soon as you attempt to put a box around Him, He will show you that He doesn't fit in it. We are taking the pages of this book to just catch a glimpse of God, but be assured, He is bigger. At the very moment you feel His power can only reach so far, that is when He will step over that boundary. At the moment you think He could never love you for what you have done, that is when He will extend his infinite and boundless love upon your repentant heart. It is at *that moment* you will profoundly realize that God is far greater than what you can possibly perceive. We might make these assumptions when considering the voice of God as well. In the previous chapters, we looked at the *might* of God through His voice—His voice of power that creates and the thunderous voice in the storm. What we are going to find in this chapter is that God does not need to utter His voice with the force of nature; He does not need the thunder, the lightning, or the earthquake. We are going to look at the story of God speaking to Elijah, and therein we will see that God maintains all power and supremacy even when He speaks softly:

> And the word of the Lord came to him: "What are you doing here, Elijah?"

> He replied, "I have been very zealous for the Lord God Almighty. The Israelites have rejected your covenant, torn down your altars, and put your prophets to death with the sword. I am the only one left, and now they are trying to kill me too."

> The Lord said, "Go out and stand on the mountain in the presence of the Lord, for the Lord is about to pass by."

Then a great and powerful wind tore the mountains apart and shattered the rocks before the Lord, but the Lord was not in the wind. After the wind, there was an earthquake, but the Lord was not in the earthquake. After the earthquake came a fire, but the Lord was not in the fire. And after the fire came a gentle whisper. When Elijah heard it, he pulled his cloak over his face and went out and stood at the mouth of the cave (1 Kgs 19:9b–13a).

It would have taken a keen observation by Elijah to notice the voice of God. Theology and history would have insisted that God was in wind, earthquake, or fire. After all, Elijah would have been acutely aware of Moses and the events that took place in the days of old. Perhaps that was the first thought of Elijah when he heard the wind and saw the mountain torn apart. Remembering the story of the ten plagues in Egypt and how God parted the Red Sea, surely it was in the wind that Elijah would hear his God speak—he heard nothing. Perhaps when Elijah felt the earthquake, that is when he was sure he would hear the voice of God. After all, everyone knows the story of when God spoke to Moses on Mount Sinai; the mountain shook and there was lightning and thundering. Elijah wasn't about to flatter himself, but perhaps that was such an event. Surely God would come with the earthquake as He did before—Elijah did not hear God in the earthquake. Then the fire came—this has to be it. Elijah would have known well the story when God consumed the outskirts of the camp of Israel with fire (Num 11) and especially the time when fire consumed 250 men during the rebellion of Korah, Dathan, and Abiram (Num 16). Fire was a symbol of power, surely God was in the fire—Elijah did not hear the voice of God in the fire.

It is easy for us, at least me, to imagine God speaking in the wind, earthquake, and fire; those elements resemble power. When you watch an action/sci-fi movie, the superhero and villain are often empowered with some force of nature: Thor could harness the power of the lightning; Magneto could manipulate metal; the Phoenix in X-Men could control fire; and many more. The list is endless of superheroes, fictitious characters that we have created to fascinate our minds as we watch them use their powers. Our imaginations appreciate that and simply are stimulated by such a storyline. Furthermore, there are times a superhero might lose his or her power and therefore cannot control that element; they are nothing without that force. I guess what I am trying to say is that our imaginations desire showy acts of power because we enjoy being entertained. And as we have seen in the previous chapters, there are times God has demonstrated His power for us to see and know Him. However, God does not need to prove His power with a supernatural act, nor has He come to entertain. There are times when God simply expects you to know that He is God.

Elijah was standing there watching these cosmic events take place right before his eyes. Each time, I think he was amazed that God did not come with the force of the wind, the shaking of the earthquake, or the heat of the fire. I think many of us would choose one of those as our entrance—such a display of power would not cease to amaze any onlooker. Furthermore, such a cosmic display of power would be a worthy introduction to God. But Elijah knew something about God that, although he might have been amazed that God did not speak in the first three events, he still did not seem startled that God came in the stillness and quietness of a whisper. Elijah knew something about God that I am attempting to bring to our attention in these pages.

We come to the most important question; what does this story tell us about our God? We have already been dancing around the answer, but allow me to be more clear. I believe our perception of God has dwindled to an unhealthy level over the past years. What I mean is that most people do not imagine a *big* God, rather their view of God is small. We, therefore, stop "going to church," we stop praying, we stop fearing—our lives become far from God-centered. I believe I may be able to put my finger on why this has happened. We don't have outward demonstrations of God commanding the wind or shaking the earth, or stirring the fires as He did in past days. Yet because of this, we quickly forget who He is and how mighty He is. I want to propose that He is so mighty that He does not have to prove Himself. Yet, in fact, He already has proven Himself when He set the foundations of the earth, and set the stars in their place, and gave the waters their boundaries. He has already proven Himself, and now when He does speak only in a soft voice, we know—we know He is the Almighty God.

PART 2: THE PRESENCE OF GOD

I happen to be a *Star Wars* fan. Don't judge me, I know a good movie when I see it. However, I am not talking about the new ones, but the original three. There is just something about the three originals that is different than the rest. The point however is the aura they put around Darth Vader. You never see him walk in a room just as anyone else; everyone stands, they tremble, they dare not disappoint. Even the music changes. If you were not in an eyeshot of the TV, you could hear it, you could tell when Darth Vader was walking in. The very presence of Darth Vader was intimidating.

Even in the non-fiction world, we understand the idea of a person's presence. As a child, it might have been when *dad* walked in the door from a long day at work. As an adult, it might be when the corporate supervisor was in the office closely examining each employee's work. Sometimes government officials have the same impact. Many get a chance to shake the hand of the president and often find it to be an honor. There are some in life who apprehend an amount of respect that makes their very presence become a thing to be feared or sought after.

In the following chapters, we are going to consider the magnitude of the presence of God. The presence of God was experienced in such a different way than it is today. The unfortunate downfall to that is that we usually allow that to impact our understanding of God—since we do not experience Him in such a real way as we read about in Scripture, He is sometimes not perceived as real. But I believe these accounts in the following chapters have been handed down to us for a clear purpose to teach us the true nature of God. And although we may experience Him in different ways, He is still the same God that we are about to read about.

4

THE CLOUD OF GLORY

The next day the whole Israelite community grumbled against Moses and Aaron. "You have killed the Lord's people," they said. But when the assembly gathered in opposition to Moses and Aaron and turned toward the tent of meeting, suddenly the cloud covered it and the glory of the Lord appeared (Num 16:41–42).

The people came before Moses and Aaron with a complaint as they often did. They were very dissatisfied with how God had been doing things, they were unhappy with Moses and Aaron, and they came before them to state their grievance. The last couple of days in the camp had been very tense, to say the least, and this was the last thing Moses wanted to hear; furthermore, this was the last thing God was willing to tolerate. Moses was immediately terrified for the people, knowing that their complaint would stir the anger of the Lord—anger that was very recently seen in a horrific way. Moses wished he had time to talk to the people to persuade them to reconsider their actions, but it was too late. As soon as the words fell from their mouths, Moses and Aaron looked behind them, and with horror they saw, toward the tent of meeting, a cloud of smoke forming—God had arrived.

I have a vivid image in my mind of this moment. The scene of this cloud forming out of nothing fascinates me. It was only supposed to be a complaint taken before Moses and Aaron. No one had even called on God yet. The morning was still young with much on the agenda. The first order of business for the community was to go to Moses and Aaron and speak of the injustices they witnessed in their leadership. Things would not go as they had planned, rather they were about to bring terror upon themselves. How did they get to this point? It did not take much to move the Israelites to complain, but this was different. For the context of this event, we need to look earlier in the chapter and meet three men who started a rebellion:

> Korah son of Izhar, the son of Kohath, the son of Levi, and certain Reubenites—Dathan and Abiram, sons of Eliab, and On son of Peleth—became insolent and rose up against Moses. With them were 250 Israelite men, well-known community leaders who had been appointed members of the council. They came as a group to oppose Moses and Aaron and said to them, "You have gone too far! The whole community is holy, every one of them, and the Lord is with them. Why then do you set yourselves above the Lord's assembly?" (Num 16:1–3).

Korah, Dathan, and Abiram were three Levites in the congregation of Israel; remember the Levites were set apart for God and with a special purpose. But these three men wanted more—I am saying this because this truly is how the story began. About 15,000 people would lose their lives because these men were not satisfied with what God had given them. They wanted to serve also in the priesthood and have Moses and Aaron share their power. But that was not what God had planned for them; each member had a role and an inheritance given to them by God. Discontent with the portion God gave them, Korah, Dathan, and Abiram were jealous of the power Moses and Aaron had. Moses did what any good leader would, he told them they will all meet in the morning and stand before God; there, God would decide.

Have you ever stood and just waited for God? I have. Sometimes it is hard to know what to expect because we live in a different realm than God—we are barrier by the flesh. But there have been times when God, in his spiritual substance, would penetrate through the fleshly curtain, and with His glory, became physically evident to everyone—this was one of those days.

Korah, Dathan, and Abiram, with all their followers, present themselves before Moses. They were all waiting and eagerly anticipating the approval of God. Can you imagine the surprise these men faced; they thought God would honor their request and that Moses had truly gone too far. Suddenly, a cloud begins to form and they watch as they know this was the moment. This was not an ordinary moment, nor was this an arrival of any ordinary person. Only *One* could arouse the stability of nature in such a way simply upon their arrival—God had come down.

It was a dreadful and terrible day stirred by the rebellion of these three men—Korah, Dathan, and Abiram. They were standing there with their families waiting for the approval of God. Eagerly desiring the power, the title, more responsibilities, and new purpose—they waited. But what happened next was not the response they expected. The ground opened up and swallowed them, their households, and all their possessions. Immediately after, fire came from God, and it consumed their followers who were there offering incense. It was not that they hadn't seen such power displayed by God before. But for the first time, it was against *them*. The people were terrified.

It was one of those days you stand there wondering what just happened. You would have to imagine that without the use of modern social media, many within the camp did not even have a clue why this horrific incident had taken place. They stood and watched, some listened to the screams, as their fellow Israelites were swallowed by the earth and others consumed by fire. It was as if the day had been consumed along with them. But the next day would be filled with horrors of its own—horrors that several thousand Israelites would not walk away from.

The next day the people of Israel came to Moses and Aaron with a complaint, accusing them of killing God's people. Little did they know that if it was not for Moses interceding on behalf of them and begging for mercy, they all would have been wiped clean from the face of the earth by God. But there they were, in their ignorance and obstinance, they were again complaining. How anyone could imagine this going well, I do not know, but sometimes the flesh gets the best of people.

The anger of God was immediately kindled. People sometimes mistake God for one who is quickly angered. Be mindful that if you were to read the story of Israel coming out of Egypt, you will find a people that were continually showered upon by God's blessings, while they complained and murmured around every corner. Given the situation, God had a right to be angry. He ignored their foolishness many times, and in more cases than can be counted He was found to be merciful. The cloud began to form—in more ways than one, the day was growing darker.

When the cloud began to form, Moses and Aaron knew—they did not know what was about to befall the people, but they knew something horrific was about to happen. I suspect they both were quickly reminded of the previous day that started the same—a complaining disgruntle people, a forming cloud, a horror. In hopes that maybe they could change the trajectory of events, Moses and Aaron both ran to the tent of meeting and stood before God where they heard the most dreadful news at which they both fell face down:

> But when the assembly gathered in opposition to Moses and Aaron and turned toward the tent of meeting, suddenly the cloud covered it and the glory of the Lord appeared. Then Moses and Aaron went to the front of the tent of meeting, and the Lord said to Moses, "Get away from this assembly so I can put an end to them at once." And they fell facedown.
>
> Then Moses said to Aaron, "Take your censor and put incense in it, along with burning coals from the altar, and hurry to the assembly to make atonement for them. Wrath has come out from the Lord; the plague has started." So Aaron did as Moses said, and ran into the midst of the assembly. The plague had already started among the people, but Aaron offered the incense and made atonement for them. He stood between the living and the dead, and the plague stopped. But 14,700 people died from the plague, in addition to those who had died because of Korah. Then Aaron returned to Moses at the entrance to the tent of meeting, for the plague had stopped (Num 16:42–50).

There are many things that can be taken from this story, but when I read through the events, I cannot grasp the fullness of the image of the cloud forming. In times of blessing and peace with God, a cloud forming would be a positively marvelous scene—look at my God! Consider His amazing glory! Perhaps that was the initial thought of Korah, Dathan, and Abiram when they saw the cloud—"God is here to defend our cause." But when a cloud begins to form due to the wrath of God, it quickly becomes a most dreadful day.

It marvels me that at the very presence of God, nature responds by proclaiming His glory—billows of smoke rise. To none other will nature respond in this way. To none other will nature proclaim His glory, but that of its Creator.

5

WOE TO ME—I AM RUINED

In the year that King Uzziah died, I saw the Lord, high and exalted, seated on a throne; and the train of His robe filled the temple. Above Him were seraphim, each with six wings: With two wings they covered their faces, with two they covered their feet, and with two they were flying. And they were calling to one another:

"Holy, holy, holy is the Lord Almighty; the whole earth is full of His glory." At the sound of their voices the door posts and thresholds shook and the temple was filled with smoke.

"Woe to me!" I cried. "I am ruined! For I am a man of unclean lips, and I live among a people of unclean lips, and my eyes have seen the King, the Lord Almighty" (Isa 6:1–5).

Isaiah is considered one of the major prophets, but the simple fact is that this is mostly due to the size of document we have preserved. Otherwise, he was as any other ordinary prophet—Isaiah would have told you nothing to the contrary. The life of Isaiah was no different than the other prophets. All things considered, Isaiah had a less exciting story to tell than most—consider Elijah with Mount Carmel, and then a few days later on Mount Horeb, or being taken up in the chariot of God. Consider Hosea, who had to live out his message to the rebellious nation of Israel, being directed by God to go marry a prostitute to show Israel their ways. Consider Daniel, who spent the night with lions. Consider Jeremiah, who would write volumes as well as Ezekiel. However, at the point in history where this story begins, Isaiah did not have much for a resume. He only had one small vision—hardly enough to even be considered a *minor* prophet. But life was about to change for this simple young man. Isaiah was about to stand in awe before the one who he dare not stand. Thinking his life was over, Isaiah was unaware that it was only about to begin.

It was the year that King Uzziah died. This introduction was intended to be more than a timestamp. Uzziah was a good king who had reigned for 52 years in the kingdom of Judah. He was a godly man. But it was now the year that he died. Even though his son Jotham would succeed him and lead as a godly man as well, things would be different when a ruler of 52 years dies.

Isaiah was in the temple. This was likely the temple of Solomon built about 200 years prior. The temple was a glorious building. Solomon imported materials from all over the world—the temple was intended to be nothing less than a splendor. Isaiah was in that temple now worshiping the Lord. But then the unexpected happens—Isaiah saw the Lord.

You might respond quickly and comment that this was in the Old Testament with the prophets. Furthermore, many will contend that we will never have a scene like this today. I have no disagreement with either statement; however, it is also because of these quick responses that we forget that one thing has not changed since this story—our God.

It is true that we do not have the *temple* as they did, and we do not have *prophets* as they did. But we have something much richer to absorb from this story. If we are able to look past the Old Testament scenery, we can see a timeless God. I want to take a few moments to try—just try—to imagine this scene. But with only one motive: to see our God for who He is and always has been. And although I will never see God seated before me with His flowing and glorious train streaming through the church while in this earthly life, I know that He still is that glorious God. I will see that train one day. We all will see that train one day when we see Him on His throne.

The first words uttered from the mouth of Isaiah when he saw the Lord is that He was *high* and *exalted*. It might have been the previous knowledge Isaiah had of the Almighty, but I think those words may also have best reflected that very moment. Furthermore, I am inclined to think that as Isaiah put sound to those words, they carried no weight to the glory that was before him. No words could have voiced what Isaiah saw. Isaiah saw God seated on a throne.

I have seen many thrones in my lifetime. I have seen thrones in movies, I have read about and have seen thrones from modern kings. I have read about ancient thrones and those of kings in the Bible. However, it pulls me out of my comprehensive ability to imagine what this throne would have looked like. A throne worthy to seat the Creator, the God of the Universe—I am lost for a picture. Yet, when Isaiah saw this throne with God sitting on it, his first words were *high* and *exalted*. Yet God allowed His Son to sit on a donkey as He rode into Jerusalem, and the people cried out,

"Hosanna, Hosanna in the highest." So I am left with no idea of what the throne looked like. Perhaps the reason we have no detail of the throne is that Isaiah was too mesmerized by the glory of God Himself. There God was seated on a throne —was it gold, wood, or metal? Isaiah did not notice or care. He was ruined either way.

Isaiah saw, flowing from God's garment, a train. A train in itself speaks of glory. All Isaiah would have had to write was that God had a train on His garment, and we would have seen His glory. However, what Isaiah saw in that moment was more than any train or robe that any ordinary king would wear. The train Isaiah saw flowing from the throne of God filled the temple. A moment prior, the temple was empty, only Isaiah and the temple articles. The air was dark and dimly lit by candles. But in that moment that Isaiah would remember for all his days, he looked around, corner to corner, from the floor to the ceiling, flowing through the whole temple, the glorious train of the Lord.

There were angels flying over the throne, each with six wings. We read of angels on many occasions through the Bible. Commonly, we know of angels to be God's messengers. Angels are seen on many occasions in the Old Testament making special visitations; Isaiah himself may have seen an angel before. But when Isaiah looked at these angels flying over the throne of God, he likely noticed that these were not ordinary angels. In no other place do I read of six-winged angels. I believe this is truly what Isaiah saw, but that is the point; what Isaiah saw was something rather peculiar. And there they were, in the sight of Isiah, flying around the throne.

The angles were speaking to one another. We must remember at this point that Isaiah was in the quiet temple worshiping. As he began to see this phenomenon before him, he heard the celestial voices of the angels ringing out as they said over and over again; "Holy, holy, holy is the Lord Almighty; the whole earth is full of his glory." What else would they say? What else would they utter continuously as they flew around the throne of the Almighty? God is holy. God is Almighty. The whole earth is full of His glory. I can type these words, and you can read them, but when they are uttered into the air from the messengers of God, the thick walls of the temple of Solomon could not withstand such a force. The air could not maintain its form from such powerful words. Creation felt the impact of its Creator as He sat there on the throne. The temple shook and was filled with smoke.

Can we bring ourselves to imagine that moment? Isaiah was in the quiet temple worshipping alone. Immediately, he sees God on a throne, the train of His robe flowing through the temple, peculiar angels flying over the throne, and when they speak everything shakes and the temple is filled with smoke. I think Isaiah's response was appropriate, for it was at that moment that he realized he was standing before the Almighty God. The humble response of any Godly man would be the same—Woe is me.

There have been times when people have forgotten the holiness of God. There have been times when some thought they could compete with the knowledge of God, or the might of God. Each time was always a humbling experience for the one contending. Isaiah was not about to contend with God or challenge Him in any way. Furthermore, Isaiah understood clearly that he was not even worthy to stand in such a room with God. The problem was that he did not have a choice in the matter—God just showed up. Isaiah was left with one thought, I am undone, I am ruined—I am a dead man.

God did not have to reveal Himself to Isaiah as one seated on a throne, but He did. God did not have to have the angels flying around, but they were. God did not have to cause the temple to tremble or be filled with smoke, but it was. God did not have to do any of these; God could have been a burst of light as was the experience of Saul of Tarsus on the road to Damascus. God shows Himself to Isaiah in a way that reveals one glory upon another. Not just a throne, but a train, and angels, and quaking, and smoke. Why?

We ask why as if God exerted all His power at that moment in the temple with Isaiah. The reality is that God hardly flinched. God could have caused the sun to be darkened, and yet not have exhausted His power. God could have created a world right there in the view of Isaiah, and yet not have exhausted His power. But all He does is sits on the throne and let His glory speak for itself.

Before the Almighty God—Woe to all humanity.

6

THE MOUNTAIN OF GLORY

There have been moments in history that become defining icons; moments that later generations look back upon and remember with awe and reverence. Moses going up to Mount Sinai would become one of these pivotal points in history. Before the mountain experience, the children of Israel were a people with no law or ethical standard to live; all they had was what they learned while in Egypt. Needless to say, those standards were not at par with God's. After Moses spent time on Mount Sinai, they would become a people with direction, with purpose, with *law*.

The children of Israel would receive something of even greater value on that day than two tablets—they would receive a fresh and new revelation of the God of Abraham:

On the morning of the third day there was thunder and lightning, with a thick cloud over the mountain, and a very loud trumpet blast. Everyone in the camp trembled. Then Moses led the people out of the camp to meet with God, and they stood at the foot of the mountain. Mount Sinai was covered with smoke, because the Lord descended on it in fire. The smoke billowed up from it like smoke from a furnace, and the whole mountain trembled violently. As the sound of the trumpet grew louder and louder, Moses spoke and the voice of God answered him (Exod 19:16–19).

They needed this! This was precisely what the children of Israel needed coming out of Egypt. It had been several hundred years since the days of the fathers of faith: Abraham, Isaac, and Jacob. Each of these forefathers had a personal knowledge of the Almighty God; each knew who God was and was declared man of faith:

> By faith Abraham, when called to go to a place he would later receive as his inheritance, obeyed and went, even though he did not know where he was going. By faith he made his home in the promised land like a stranger in a foreign country; he lived in tents, as did Isaac and Jacob, who were heirs with him of the same promise … . By faith Abraham, when God tested him, offered Isaac as a sacrifice. He who had embraced the promises was about to sacrifice his one and only son.

> By faith Isaac blessed Jacob and Esau in regard to their future.

> By faith Jacob, when he was dying, blessed each of Joseph's sons, and worshiped as he leaned on the top of his staff (Heb 11:8–9, 17, 20–21).

But during the time of Moses, these men had become mere legendary stories for most. For some these stories might have been full of sincere theological substance, but for others, perhaps just a story they read to their children before bed. The children of Israel needed this experience at the base of the mountain.

Furthermore, the children of Israel had been living in Egypt for roughly 400 years. When they first arrived in Egypt, life was easy, lines were clearly drawn, and favor was on their side. Jacob and his family, seventy members in all, traveled to Egypt at the invitation of Joseph due to the great famine in the land. When they arrived, they were given the land of Goshen to live in, which was just on the northern side of Egypt. Things went great for a while. The Pharaoh was favorable to Joseph, the man who singlehandedly saved the land. Joseph had his family with him again, they all had food—they could ask for nothing more. However, when Joseph died, and also the after the death of the Pharaoh who supported Joseph, life changed greatly. The seventy members of Jacob's family quickly grew, and with that, the Egyptians became afraid of the potential threat this small family of Joseph's had become. In response, the Egyptians forced the children of Israel into slavery as a means to keep them under control. For many years, a few hundred to be more clear, life was misery.

The reason I am writing this is to help us see the conditions in which the children of Israel lived for the four hundred years prior to the Mount Sinai experience. However, the suffering as slaves was really the least of their worries at this time. They knew hardships even before they came to Egypt. The biggest threat was becoming culturized to Egyptian ways, practices, and theology. They were living in a pagan land under pagan leadership. Even after a mere one-hundred years, they would have been greatly impacted; adopting new principles, and changing with culture. After two hundred years, values would be compromised, covenants forgotten, and new covenants made. After three hundred years, generations would be forgotten, forefathers would become stories and myths. After four hundred years, they would be an entirely different people than the seventy who came in—different in many ways. Some might have known of the legendary story of Abraham's faith on the mountain with Isaac, but that faith faded into history with Abraham. The children of Israel have not really known God for quite a while.

The children of Israel needed to see God and His fierce might on the mountain—they needed to learn and be reminded of who the God of Israel was. We see the evidence of this need even as early as when Moses first returned to talk to Pharaoh. Because of Pharaoh's irritation toward Moses, the labor was increased, and the people immediately complained to Moses. We see the evidence of this need when they complained at the Red Sea and at the waters of Marah, thinking God brought them out into the desert just to kill them. This happened on several occasions even before they arrived at Mount Sinai. We can see the evidence of the need for a new revelation of God when their immediate response to thinking Moses was killed on the mountain was to build an idol to the likings of what they remembered in Egypt. The first couple of weeks of leaving Egypt, it was quite evident, the children of Israel have long forgotten just who their God was—at Mount Sinai, they would be reminded. Will they change overnight? Absolutely not. But they will receive a fresh glimpse of the Almighty.

There they were, in a moment that seemed like a nightmare. They had become aware of many of the lifeless gods of Egypt over the past several hundred years. Some of the children of Israel likely were worshipers of these gods as well.

But those gods sat on the shelf. Those gods were carved with their own hands. Those gods had to be handled carefully to not break them if dropped. But who was this God shaking this mountain?

In a matter of just a few weeks, the children of Israel came to know the God of Abraham in a real way that would change their lives forever. As they stood at the base of Mount Sinai, they saw the lightning, and they heard the thunder. They watched as smoke engulfed the mountain. They felt the mountain quake fiercely. They became acutely aware of the Most High God, and they stood there in referent awe and in fear. Furthermore, Moses walked down from the mountain, unharmed and having a glow over his head. They realized on that day that the God of Abraham, Isaac, and Jacob was no ordinary God.

7

LIFE-GIVING DRY BONES

Now Moabite raiders used to enter the country every spring. Once while some Israelites were burying a man, suddenly they saw a band of raiders; so they threw the man's body into Elisha's tomb. When the body touched Elisha's bones, the man came to life and stood up on his feet (2 Kgs 13:20–21).

No one could have anticipated this event. No one could have possibly expected this to happen on that sad day of mourning. Even in the text, this small story is comprised of two verses that are oddly wedged in the middle of the chapter. It simply was unexpected and didn't fit. It was during the reign of King Jehoash, king of Israel. It was during those days that Elisha died. The verses that follow tell of the oppression of the land of Judah by the hand of Aram. But the writer takes a space of two verses to add the story of these raiders entering Israel. Even in the text, we are caught by surprise; where did these raiders come from, and why are we reading about them?

I would have to say that the ones who were most surprised by the events of that day were the guys carrying the body to the grave. It was a normal day, a sad day, but otherwise normal for a spring afternoon. There was a funeral procession. You might imagine the scene to look similar to the funeral Jesus embarked upon for a particular young man, the widow's son at Nain (Luke 7:11–17). There was probably family there mourning, and of course, the men carrying the dead body. The funeral Jesus crashed would not end as any expected, and neither would the funeral in the book of Kings.

A band of raiders was seen coming from a distance. Out of self-preservation, everyone would have run for safety, leaving the dead body in the hands of the men carrying it. Now in Israel, there were many caves. So, the men carrying the dead body threw the corpse into the most convenient cave and made a run for it themselves. This is where the story turns off the normal path. As we see from the text, the dead body just happened to land on the dry bones of Elisha, and consequently returns to life.

This is where the text ends, but we must allow our imaginations to run rampant for a moment to see the full picture of the peculiarity of that day. The dead man, now living and standing in the cave, would have climbed out of the cave only to see and hear a band of raiders coming quickly. This man would have also seen his friends, the ones who were recently carrying his dead body, running toward town a few hundred feet ahead. So this man who was just raised to life would have started running towards his friends to save his own life. What a sight that would have been for his friends. Not only were they running from a band of raiders, but they turn back and saw their friend running behind them as well, their friend who should've been lying dead in the cave where they tossed him. A strange day to say the least.

What just happened there? I imagine them all talking back in town about the event. But what would their answers be? I am sure they speculated many theories, but the answer would not be clear until they returned to the scene of the event. The raiders would have returned home with their plunder allowing these men to safely return. They didn't go to where the man was supposed to be buried; that grave, oddly enough, wouldn't be filled for a few years yet. But they returned to that grave which would have seemed like a random cave in the spare of the moment when running for your life as they were. But when they looked closer, the answer was clear. It was remarkable, it was inconceivable, but it was clear. In the cave lay the bones of the prophet Elisha.

Who was Elisha? No man could be accredited such power without reason. Never before has any man received breathe into his lungs simply by falling upon dry bones. It is when we learn who Elisha was and the power of God that was upon him that things will begin to make sense. We first meet Elisha in First Kings 19 when he receives the call from Elijah.

So Elijah went from there and found Elisha son of Shaphat. He was plowing with twelve yoke of oxen, and he himself was driving the twelfth pair. Elijah went up to him and threw his cloak around him. Elisha then left his oxen and ran after Elijah. "Let me kiss my father and mother good-bye," he said, "and then I will come with you."

"Go back," Elijah replied. "What have I done to you?"

So Elisha left him and went back. He took his yoke of oxen and slaughtered them. He burned the plowing equipment to cook the meat and gave it to the people, and they

ate. Then he set out to follow Elijah and became his servant
(1 Kgs 19:19–21).

This is the last we hear of Elisha until he succeeds Elijah
in 2 Kings 2. All we do know from these hidden years is that
Elisha served Elijah, who was a great prophet in Israel. We
read of many amazing miracles performed by Elijah through
the chapters of the Kings. Elijah is even mentioned several
times in the New Testament by Jesus, James, and Paul.
Furthermore, on the Mount of Transfiguration, it was none
other than Moses and Elijah who appeared before Jesus
(Matt 17). Elijah was renowned through the land as being a
great prophet of God, and to finish the matter, he did not
even face death but was taken into heaven by a chariot of
fire. But what does this tell us about Elisha?

On the day that Elijah was to be taken up to heaven, he
told Elisha to stay where they were as he headed by himself
to Bethel. Needless to say, Elisha refused as he insisted to
stay with his master, his mentor. Several times Elijah told
Elisha to stay, but each time he refused. Finally, the moment
came; as they crossed the Jordan river, Elisha was asked a
question that would change his life.

> When they had crossed, Elijah said to Elisha, "Tell me, what
> can I do for you before I am taken from you?" "Let me
> inherit a double portion of your spirit," Elisha replied. "You
> have asked a difficult thing." Elijah said, "yet if you see me
> when I am taken from you, it will be yours—otherwise, it
> will not" (2 Kgs 2:9–10).

Elisha was asked an open-ended question, "What do you
want?" Much can be said about the character of a person
when asked a question like this. We see a similar situation in

1 Kings 3 when God asked Solomon a question when he first became king. In the story of Solomon, the question was open and the options were limited only by his imagination. Would he choose riches, fame, or good health? No, the one thing Solomon requested from the Lord was a discerning heart to govern the people. In a like manner, Elijah asked Elisha what he could do for him before he departed. Elisha's answer spoke volumes of what kind of man he was and also set a course for who he would become.

A double portion of your spirit. Elisha did not ask for wealth and fame. But as he served Elijah, he was able to see the power of God as it changed the lives of so many people. Elisha wanted that power. He did not want the power for himself; I believe Elisha wanted to impact the lives of people as Elijah did. But Elisha didn't only want to be *like* his master, he wanted more. I believe his motives were quite pure, and that is why it was honored by God. *Don't only give me what you have, I want a double portion.*

What does a double portion of the spirit of Elijah look like? Said simply, I believe it is a remarkable manifestation of power. It is a phenomenal outpouring of the power of God. What does a person do when they are given such power from God? If you are Elisha, you pour yourself out to serve others and do miracles. And as you might expect from a *double* portion, Elisha did twice as many miracles as Elijah. Furthermore, there was only one person who walked upon the earth who was recorded to have done more miracles than Elisha, and that was Jesus Christ Himself. So what does a double portion of the spirit of Elijah look like?—Power.

We now have to return to 2 Kings 13. This is the intriguing part of the story because Elisha eventually died. We are not sure how long he was dead, but nonetheless, he was dead and buried in a cave. He was gifted with such immense power from God that even after death, the power was still soaked into his bones. But remember from earlier chapters, God's power is a creative power and life-giving. It was God's unfathomable power that created the worlds by just a spoken word and the moving of the Holy Spirit. It was that same power that was still resting upon the bones of Elisha. With all that being said, now it makes sense. What else would we expect to happen when a dead body fell upon such power of God—Life!

This is telling of our God. It further helps us to understand His power, that even after Elisha took his final breath, the power was present and active. But what interests me the most is the life-giving nature of the power. The story could have gone in many directions, but it takes the course of revealing to us the foremost nature of our God as the giver of life.

In Luke 8, we are introduced to a woman with an issue with her blood; she was dying. She had exhausted all of her resources and was left with no hope. One day she heard Jesus was coming through town. Her response was remarkable. She didn't want His attention. She didn't demand an audience with Him. She needed healing; she desired her life. There was something about Jesus that this woman thought to herself, *all I have to do is touch the hem of His garment.* She pressed through the crowd, exhausting the last bit of energy she had, but she finally was able to just touch the hem. Immediately, flowing into her body, there was healing and life. Again, this is quite telling of our God. If this is what happens with just a touch, what do you think can happen if He lived in your heart?

8

THE ARK OF GOD

There are some things in life that are blessings, and there are some that are curses. We handle each accordingly; the things that are blessed are valued and everyone wants it. The cursed objects we try to tuck away. But when you have an object that is both a blessing and a curse, the utmost care is needed. This was the case with the Ark of the Covenant. For therein were life, prosperity, and hope. But also, molded within the intricate gold design was the curse of death.

When Moses came out of Egypt with the children of Israel, they came to Mount Sinai. On the mountain, Moses was given the two tablets containing the law. With that, he was also given instructions to build a tabernacle with articles of worship therein. It was an exciting time for Israel. Not only were they free, not only did they have a God to worship, but now they were going to have a *place* of worship. Not only that, and even more exciting was that God was going to dwell with them.

There were three sections in the tabernacle. Within the

first section of the tabernacle of Moses, the outer court, there was the bronze altar and the bronze wash basin. Within the next section, the holy place; on the right, there was the table of showbread, on the left was the golden candlesticks, and straight ahead was the altar of incense. Directly behind the altar of incense was the door to the most holy place, the place only the high priest was allowed to go only once a year. Within the holy place was the ark of the covenant:

And they shall make an ark of acacia wood; two and a half cubits shall be its length, a cubit and a half its width, and a cubit and a half its height. And you shall overlay it with pure gold, inside and out you shall overlay it, and shall make on it a molding of gold all around. You shall cast four rings of gold for it, and put them in its four corners; two rings shall be on one side, and two rings on the other side. And you shall make poles of acacia wood, and overlay them with gold. You shall put the poles into the rings on the sides of the ark, that the ark may be carried by them. The poles shall be in the rings of the ark; they shall not be taken from it. And you shall put into the ark the Testimony which I will give you.

You shall make a mercy seat of pure gold; two and a half cubits shall be its length and a cubit and a half its width. And you shall make two cherubim of gold; of hammered work you shall make them at the two ends of the mercy seat. Make one cherub at one end, and the other cherub at the other end; you shall make the cherubim at the two ends of it of one piece with the mercy seat. And the cherubim shall stretch out their wings above, covering the mercy seat with their wings, and they shall face one another; the faces of the cherubim shall be toward the mercy seat. You shall put the mercy seat on top of the ark, and in the ark you shall put the Testimony that I will give you. And there I will meet with you, and I will speak with you from above the mercy seat, from between the two cherubim which are on the ark of the Testimony, about everything which I will give you in commandment to the children of Israel" (Exod 25:10–22).

The ark was not simply another piece of furniture. While all the other things in the tabernacle were sacred, they were still just pieces of furniture, but not the ark. The ark was made special. On top of the ark was placed the mercy seat, also called the atonement cover. Hovering over the mercy seat were the wings of two cherubim. It was upon that seat that God promised to dwell. In verse 22, He said, "And there I will meet with you, and I will speak with you from above the mercy seat, from between the two cherubim which are on the ark of the Testimony." It was a very special yet terrifying time for Israel. Their God, the one true God, desired to dwell with them. He would reside within the camp with them. He would sit upon the ark of the covenant. They would learn, with time and amazement, how special this was. At the same time, they would learn how terrifying it was to have God dwell in their midst.

We have a saying that you cannot put God in a box. Although God did place His presence upon the ark of the covenant, it was man's inability to handle such power. At first, and how God designed it, the ark with His presence on it was to be an object of worship—not the box, yet His presence residing upon it. It truly was a blessed time to have their God so near and to have worship so accessible. They were continually reminded of the reverence required. As we saw before, it was only the high priest who could go before the ark only once a year. And that was after he performed upon himself arduous cleansing ceremonies. To go before the presence of God was a great and terrible thing, for the presence of God was so great.

Over the course of time, moving forward to the days of Eli, things changed. The ark of the covenant had been in Israel for about 500; this is a lot of time for values to shift. The ark was still kept in a sacred place, But the worship was not what it used to be. Somewhere down the line, the power of God shifted from being an object of worship to merely becoming a weapon. Now it is true that even during the time of Moses, the ark went into battle with them. But it was a symbol of sending God into the battle to be the victor. The respect and reverence were there, the worship was there. God was their God and Victor. But time has a way of changing things

As with any form of worship, things had changed over the few hundred years until the time of Eli. During those many years, we see the ark of the Lord fewer times than we should. Joshua used the ark when first entering the promised land, but after that, the ark was only mentioned once in a span of nearly 500 years. There is something that should be noticed about that. The ark was once a symbol of the presence of God; in fact, it was more than a symbol, for the very presence of God rested upon the ark. The ark was, for all intents and purposes, the center of their lives. But when that ark was mentioned so seldom in such a span of time, it is evident that the awe and reverence had dissipated. The ark, which was once the center of worship, became a mere piece of furniture—and a weapon.

During the days of Eli, Israel was at war with the Philistines. Before they had thought to take the ark with them, they went out to battle alone. Perhaps their thoughts were that they could handle the fight without the help of

God. But when they went without their God, they also forfeited their victory. It was only when they had lost the battle that they thought to go get the ark:

> Now the Israelites went out to fight against the Philistines. The Israelites camped at Ebenezer, and the Philistines at Aphek. The Philistines deployed their forces to meet Israel, and as the battle spread, Israel was defeated by the Philistines, who killed about four thousand of them on the battlefield. When the soldiers returned to camp, the elders of Israel asked, "Why did the Lord bring defeat on us today before the Philistines? Let us bring the ark of the Lord's covenant from Shiloh, so that He may go with us and save us from the hand of our enemies."
>
> So the people sent men to Shiloh, and they brought back the ark of the covenant of the Lord Almighty, who is enthroned between the cherubim. And Eli's two sons, Hophni and Phinehas, were there with the ark of the covenant of God (1 Sam 4:1–4).

We can quickly see that there was evident knowledge of the power of God in the ark of the covenant, but there had grown in the hearts of the Israelites a callus to His presence. During its days of inauguration, the ark was placed in the middle of the camp so that God would likewise be the center of their lives. For a while, He was. For a while, the respect and reverent awe remained. But time does what time always does—it erodes.

The ark was once an object of worship. It was the glory of Israel, the people in which whose God dwelt among them. Nations feared, and Israel rejoiced. But those days had long passed. The ark had become a piece of furniture that was only brought out *if needed*. The Israelites had no interest in the ark until they lost the battle. It was at that point that they got the ark. They loaded it up and hauled it into the camp as if it were a war machine designed for mass destruction. The respect for the box which they carried was long lost. God was faithful, but the people's hearts were far from Him. The people's response is quite telling:

> And when the ark of the covenant of the Lord came into the camp, all Israel shouted so loudly that the earth shook. Now when the Philistines heard the noise of the shout, they said, "What *does* the sound of this great shout in the camp of the Hebrews *mean?*" Then they understood that the ark of the Lord had come into the camp. So the Philistines were afraid, for they said, "God has come into the camp!"
>
> And they said, "Woe to us! For such a thing has never happened before. Woe to us! Who will deliver us from the hand of these mighty gods? These *are* the gods who struck the Egyptians with all the plagues in the wilderness. Be strong and conduct yourselves like men, you Philistines, that you do not become servants of the Hebrews, as they have been to you. Conduct yourselves like men, and fight" (1 Sam 4:5–9)!

All of Israel rejoiced at the sight of the ark. But they did not rejoice because of the presence of their God but because they were going to win the battle. There was a day when the people had such regard for the ark and the presence of God. When Joshua led Israel over the Jordan and against Jericho, they sent the ark first. It was not a mere weapon; they were sending their mighty God before them. They knew that God was the victor. On that day, Israel only had to be obedient and shout as they watched the fortress of Jericho tumble. Their God sat upon the ark, and He was their God.

The ark had faced many battles, and Israel had become numb to the presence of God. What was supposed to be the glory of Israel became a secret weapon in a box that was kept in the temple. God was no longer their victory. The ark was their last stand; *if we can't win the battle, we will go fetch the ark.*

I want you to notice the different view that even the Philistines had toward the ark; they had a fear and respect for the power of God. They understood clearly that that box overlaid with gold was no ordinary box. They understood that sitting on that box was the same God who defeated the Egyptians many years ago. They understood the power of God, and they feared greatly. But they fought. Even with sure defeat ahead of them, they fought like men. The events would not end as expected for anyone:

> So the Philistines fought, Israel was defeated, and every man fled to his tent. There was a very great slaughter, and there fell of Israel thirty thousand foot soldiers. Also the ark of God was captured; and the two sons of Eli, Hophni and Phinehas, died (1 Sam 4:10–11).

This was a very traumatic day for Israel. The ark of the covenant had been stolen. Upon hearing the news of the ark being captured, Eli fell backward off his chair and died. Furthermore, Eli's daughter-in-law was pregnant. She gave birth to a son and named him *Ichabod*, saying, "The glory has departed from Israel, for the ark of God has been captured (1 Sam 4:21–22).

The Philistines took the ark of the covenant to Ashdod and placed it in the temple of Dagon. It was a victorious day to be recorded in history. They had known of the power of the ark, but to have captured it was renown. They had no idea what they had done. They had no idea the magnitude of the power sitting upon that golden box. That night, the ark of God was placed in the same room as the Philistine idol, Dagon. In 1 Samuel 5, we read that the next morning when the Philistines went into the temple, they found Dagon fallen over. Perplexed as they were, they placed the idol back upright. The next morning it was found fallen over again, but this time with its head and hands broken off. The curiosity that filled their imaginations was turning to fear. The power from the ark was so great that the people in the area began to develop tumors. They knew right away that the ark must be removed. The ark was brought into the Philistine camp as a victory trophy, but to their horror, it was becoming a dreadful curse.

The Philistines moved the ark to Gath, a neighboring Philistine city. But the power of God came upon them as well. The people were thrown into a great panic as the whole city as well had an outbreak of tumors. Fearful for their lives, they sent the ark away quickly. The ark was taken to Ekron, but they feared all the more, knowing the events that had taken place. They cried out, "Send the ark of the god of Israel away; let it go back to its own place, or it will kill us and our people." Before the horror became worse, plans were made to return the ark to Israel.

PART 3: THE TESTIMONY OF GOD

When I had my construction business, I surprisingly did not have to do hardly any advertising, and I was still getting more work than I could manage. The secret was the powerful idea of "word of mouth." My customers would tell their friends about me, they would show off their new bathroom, kitchen, or their freshly new painted house. Needless to say, their friends would call me, and the work just piled in. I don't say this to brag, but rather to draw attention to the power of what people say about another person, thing, or even God.

What a person says about oneself carries some weight, but what is said about someone by others is where the testimony gains power. We even understand this in our society today. A good example is when you try to get a job for just about any company. They will look at your resume and will call you in for an interview to allow you to tell them what you think about yourself and what you want them to know. But most companies do not hire a person solely on a person's own testimony. Companies will often call the references provided on the applicant's resume. It is not that they don't trust the applicant; they want to know what others have to say. What kind of reputation or testimony has the applicant acquired? That will get a person hired—or not.

In the following chapters, we are going to see the testimony given by others about God. Yet, if I only provided testimonies from fellow believers like myself, I don't think that will carry much value. What I did in these chapters is I found testimonies from both God-fearing men and women, but also those who did not. It is time to check the references of God; what have people said about Him?

9

RAHAB, THE HARLOT

I know that the Lord has given you this land and that a great fear of you has fallen on us, so that all who live in this country are melting in fear because of you. We have heard how the Lord dried up the water of the Red Sea for you when you came out of Egypt, and what you did to Sihon and Og, the two kings of the Amorites east of the Jordan, whom you completely destroyed. When we heard of it, our hearts melted in fear and everyone's courage failed because of you, for the Lord your God is God in heaven above and on the earth below (Josh 2:9–11).

I have always admired Rahab and the certainty with which she made her statement; "I know ... ." The children of Israel had to spend the previous thirty-eight years wandering through the wilderness to come to this conviction. Rahab asserts that she and the rest of the country were well aware of the fearful fact that the God of Israel was mighty. And furthermore, He was fighting for His people.

The passage begins with the parting of the Red Sea, but

truly the hand of God began to move even before then. I could take our minds back to the plagues upon Egypt, but we have to look beyond that as well. We really have to jump more than four hundred years prior when God orchestrated Joseph becoming a leader in Israel. But that in itself was the intricate plan to fulfill the promise God made to Abraham. I guess what I am seeing is that it was a masterful plan that brought Israel to the border of the Canaan land—the surrounding nations saw that, yet it was a faint but growing truth for Israel.

God brought the children of Israel out of Egypt with many fascinating plagues. It would seem sensible that after such a display of power when they were pinned against the Red Sea, they would have known that God was at work. But they murmured and complained that God brought them out there simply to kill them. What they failed to see was that God was doing something good.

When Israel left Egypt, they left by the way of Sukkoth and went to Etham. Looking at the map, this was a very sensible place to stop. They were just north of the Red Sea. They planned to stay the night. In the morning they would fill the water jugs, and without any foreseen interruptions, head east. However, if you play that out, there would have never been a "Red Sea" experience. If God had never parted the Red Sea, the nations would not have known and feared God the way they did. Rahab would have had a very different testimony to give if any. But read the following text carefully; you will see that God was up to something:

> After leaving Sukkoth they camped at Etham on the edge of
> the desert. By day the Lord went ahead of them in a pillar of
> cloud to guide them on their way and by night in a pillar of
> fire to give them light, so that they could travel by day or

night. Neither the pillar of cloud by day nor the pillar of fire by night left its place in front of the people.

Then the Lord said to Moses, "Tell the Israelites to turn back and encamp near Pi Hahiroth, between Migdol and the sea." They are to encamp by the sea, directly opposite Baal Zephon. Pharaoh will think, "The Israelites are wandering around the land in confusion, hemmed in by the desert." (Exod 13:20–14:3).

As we see from the text, God had Israel move from Etham and camp at Pi Hahiroth. This might not seem like a big deal at first, and probably was not noticed by the Israelites at the moment, but God was placing them on the west side of the Red Sea for a purpose—He was setting them up. When Egypt came to take back their slaves, Israel was not at Etham where they would have had an easy get-away. They were at Pi Hahiroth—trapped. It was in that moment God was wanting to show His glory for Israel and for all the nations to see. In a way that cannot fully be understood, God parted the waters, allowing Israel to cross on dry ground. This event changed the surrounding nations.

Having experienced such a powerful demonstration of their God, one might think that Israel would have marched straight to the border of Canaan with newfound confidence. But that was not quite how the story went. Upon hearing of the Red Sea, the surrounding nations, including Canaan, understood what the God of Israel was doing. They understood and trembled with fear. Israel was still a work in progress.

Just days after leaving the Red Sea, Israel was camped at the waters of Marah (Exod 15:22–27). They were very thirsty, but the water at Marah was bitter. Still not aware that God had good things planned for them, Israel again complained. God commanded Moses to throw a stick into the water, and it became good to drink. Just another sign that God had good things planned. But did you really get what just happened; Moses *threw* a stick into the water. There is no rationale that such a simple task would purify water. I believe it was God's way of saying that He can handle big problems with hardly any exertion at all. You need pure water? No problem. Just throw that stick in the water, and done. The nations around them understood that God was doing something big for the nation of Israel. Israel still had much to learn.

Not long after leaving Marah, Israel passed through Elim and came to the Desert of Sin (Exod 16). As was natural for any person, they became hungry and were without food. One would think that after seeing the plagues, the Red Sea parted, and then waters purified by a mere throw of a stick, the Israelites would have been ready to realize that their God was mighty and was mission-set to take care of them. That was not quite the case.

> The Israelites said to [Moses and Aaron], "If only we had died by the Lord's hand in Egypt! There we sat around pots of meat and ate all the food we wanted, but you have brought us out into this desert to starve this entire assembly to death" (Exod 16:3).

They had no clue what God was doing. The nations around them, at this very time were fearfully watching Israel near their land as they cross the wilderness. Meanwhile, Israel complained that Moses had brought them out to starve them all to death.

By the time Israel reached the border of Kadesh Barnea, the people of Canaan were vexed with fear with hearts melting. They planned to fight, but they expected nothing less than sure defeat. After all, who can stand against a nation whose God can part the waters of a sea? But Israel did not quite understand the magnitude of their God. When they spied out the Canaan land, they saw the giants and were afraid:

> They said, "The land we explored devours those living in it. All the people we saw there are great size. We saw the Nephilim there (descendants of Anak come from the Nephilim). We seemed like grasshoppers in our own eyes, and we looked the same to them" (Num 13:32a–33).

But they were wrong.

They saw themselves as grasshoppers because they did not factor in that a mighty God was on their side. And if they truly understood the magnitude of their God, it wouldn't matter if the enemy looked at them as grasshoppers. But therein was the problem, the enemy did *not* view them as grasshoppers. From the testimony of Rahab, who was a Canaanite harlot, the God of Israel was greatly to be feared. The whole county lost all courage as Israel neared their border. Their hearts melted in fear. Yes, it was just a group of Israelites that in and of themselves could defeat no one. But the Canaanites knew very well the magnitude of the God of Israel, and they trembled.

The day Israel turned around to head back into the wilderness for thirty-eight more years was a day the nations would never forget. It was supposed to be their demise. They all stood there in disbelief and confusion as Israel marched away carrying the defeat that was not theirs to carry. For the next thirty-eight years, the people of Canaan waited. They waited for Israel to get to know their God on a new level.

Israel had a lot of Egypt that had to be purged out of their hearts. But after the long and many years in the wilderness, after the passing of Moses, Joshua took the people to the border of Canaan near Jericho. Jericho and the rest of the land knew the time had come. The Almighty God of Israel had come to fight and their walls did not stand a chance.

There should never be a moment when the world around us understands the power of God more than God's people.

10

DAVID, THE PSALMIST

David was a man who had many highs and lows in life. I start with this because one might suspect that David could have gone either direction with his testimony about God; he could have complained about God because of all his troubles. Afterall, isn't it normal to expect God to do good things on your behalf as long as you live upright? David could have easily felt short-changed by God. But we do not see such an attitude in the writings of David. I mean, we do see a few psalms where David is outright honest with God. But I would not call that a disrespectful complaint and dissatisfaction about God. Moreover, it is an example to us that God is okay if we are honest and, with respect, express our hearts to Him—and that is what David did.

In addition to the honest expression of David's heart, we also see many psalms in which David poured out praise to God, and in some psalms, David continued to give the reason *why*. Psalms like these are gold mines for us to see into the heart of David. I chose one particular psalm to look at to get a clear view of the way David thought about God. Forgive me for jumping into a little bit of commentary style, but I think this is the best way to unveil these beautiful verses.

Psalm 18

> I love you, Lord, my strength. The Lord is my rock, my fortress and my deliverer; my God is my rock, in whom I take refuge, my shield and the horn of my salvation, my stronghold (Ps 18:1–2).

A clear statement of love and appreciation towards God. When David thought about God, he thought of a fortress, a deliverer, a rock, a shield, a horn of salvation, and a stronghold. But this testimony did not come without reason. As we are going to see in the next passage, David did not only ascribe this honor to God, but it was due to Him because of all He had done. David continued to explain in the next few verses with a backstory. In a comical way, I am reminded of Dr. Doofenshmirtz in the animated series, *Phineas and Ferb*. Every episode would follow the same plot line: Dr. Doofenshmirtz would build some crazy contraption that Perry the platypus would have to stop. Before launching the evil contraption, Dr. Doofenshmirtz would give a backstory showing what part of his childhood lead up to that moment. He always had a *why*. In the same way, David gives us the *why*. For what reason did he call God his fortress and stronghold and so on? We are about to find out—David's backstory:

> I called to the Lord, who is worthy of praise, and I have been saved from my enemies. The cords of death entangled me; the torrents of destruction overwhelmed me. The cords

of the grave coiled around me; the snares of death confronted me. In my distress I called to the Lord; I cried to my God for help (Ps 18:3–6a).

It all started with a low tide in the life of David. The superscription indicates that David wrote this psalm when the Lord delivered him from the hands of Saul. David suffered much turmoil at the hands of Saul. Ever since David was anointed king, there was contention; Saul was a very jealous king. For several years *after* David was anointed king, he was chased by Saul, who literally would have killed him if he had the chance. This psalm indicates that on this particular occasion when David was being pursued, Saul almost succeeded. Saul was so close that David considered himself entangled by death with the cords of the grave coiled around him. But at that moment when David was deprived of all hope, he cried out to the Lord. The following passage is what reveals the most beautiful nature of God:

The earth trembled and quaked, and the foundations of the mountains shook; they trembled because he was angry. Smoke rose from his nostrils; consuming fire came from his mouth, burning coals blazed out of it. He parted the heavens and came down; dark clouds were under his feet. He mounted the cherubim and flew; he soared on the wings of the wind. He made darkness his covering, his canopy around him—the dark rain clouds of the sky. Out of the brightness of his presence clouds advanced, with hailstones and bolts of lightning. The Lord thundered from heaven; the voice of the Most High resounded. He shot his arrows and scattered the enemy, with great bolts of lightning he routed them. The valleys of the sea were exposed and the foundations of the earth laid bare at your rebuke, Lord, at the blast of breath from your nostrils. He reached down from on high and took hold of me; he drew me out of deep waters. He rescued me from my powerful enemy, from my foes, who were too strong for me (Ps 18:7–17).

This scene is fascinating when you allow your imagination to do the work. David cried out to God. David was helpless, alone, in distress—he was the victim. David acknowledged that God heard his cry from His temple. But what happens next is simply awesome! There was a great earthquake throughout the world. Why? Because God was angry.

I am a bit perplexed as I consider if these events literally happened or not. If they in fact did, it would have been as in the book of Revelation, but in David's time. Some of these details make you wonder what damage was dealt to the earth, all because God was angry. My proposal is that we attempt to keep the intent of this psalm without getting lost in critiquing its reality. Because either way, we are left with the same reality—the *testimony* by David of the magnitude of God. If you think the details in this passage are literal, then David wrote of the magnitude of God as it was demonstrated clearly before his own eyes. One thing we know for sure is that God delivered David from a horrible trap of the enemy. I think the following proposal may be more accurate. At that moment when David was rescued from what he thought was sure death, he had a fresh and vivid image of the magnitude of God. God was David's fortress; He was his stronghold. Furthermore, God was so mighty that when He rose up from His throne, the entire earth trembled. Out of His mouth came consuming fire. He rode upon the clouds down to earth as the heavens opened up. I could go on through the verses, but the point is clear. David was painting for us a picture of how he saw God. And the painting rendered shows God as incomparable to any other, and that is just the point. David wanted to express in this psalm that there is no God like his.

With such a view of God, David continued to utter the praises of God and speak of His majesty. The following verses are what David had to say:

> They confronted me in the day of my disaster, but the Lord was my support. He brought me out into a spacious place; he rescued me because he delighted in me. The Lord has dealt with me according to my right-eousness; according to the cleanness of my hands he has rewarded me. For I have kept the ways of the Lord; I am not guilty of turning from my God. All his laws are before me; I have not turned away from his decrees. I have been blame-less before him and have kept myself from sin. The Lord has rewarded me according to my righteousness, according to the cleanness of my hands in his sight. To the faithful you show yourself faithful, to the blameless you show yourself blameless, to the pure you show yourself pure, but to the devious you show yourself shrewd. You save the humble but bring low those whose eyes are haughty. You, Lord, keep my lamp burning; my God turns my darkness into light. With your help I can advance against a troop; with my God I can scale a wall. As for God, his way is perfect: The Lord's word is flawless; he shields all who take refuge in him. For who is God besides the Lord? And who is the Rock except our God (Ps 18:18–31)?

David was not only aware of the power of God and being able to subdue his enemies, but David also knew of the many wonderful attributes of God. God is just and rewards the righteous. God saves the humble but brings low the haughty. God turns light into darkness. God is flawless. God shields all those who take refuge in Him. The reasonable conclusion David came to is simple: *God, there is none like You.*

And although that could have easily been the chapter ending, David had more he has to say about God:

It is God who arms me with strength and keeps my way secure. He makes my feet like the feet of a deer; he causes me to stand on the heights. He trains my hands for battle; my arms can bend a bow of bronze. You make your saving help my shield, and your right hand sustains me; your help has made me great. You provide a broad path for my feet, so that my ankles do not give way. I pursued my enemies and overtook them; I did not turn back till they were destroyed. I crushed them so that they could not rise; they fell beneath my feet. You armed me with strength for battle; you humbled my adversaries before me. You made my enemies turn their backs in flight, and I destroyed my foes. They cried for help, but there was no one to save them—to the Lord, but he did not answer. I beat them as fine as windblown dust; I trampled them like mud in the streets. You have delivered me from the attacks of the people; you have made me the head of nations. People I did not know now serve me, foreigners cower before me; as soon as they hear of me, they obey me. They all lose heart; they come trembling from their strongholds. The Lord lives! Praise be to my Rock! Exalted be God my Savior! He is the God who avenges me, who subdues nations under me, who saves me from my enemies. You exalted me above my foes; from a violent man you rescued me. Therefore, I will praise you, Lord, among the nations; I will sing the praises of your name. He gives his king great victories; he shows unfailing love to his anointed, to David and to his descendants forever (Ps 18:32–50).

It was God. God strengthened David. God delivered David. God destroyed the enemies of David. It is for these reasons that David began this chapter by calling God his fortress, his deliverer, his rock, his shield, a horn of salvation, and his stronghold. And David closes the psalm with the fervent conclusion; "Therefore, I will praise you."

There was no god more powerful or anything near equal to the one God of Jacob. David saw God as his source and sustainer of life. To David, it was not a matter *if* he needed God or not. David understood that he existed for his God and only because he was created by God. David understood that he could not go one day if it were not for God sustaining him. But all this did not trouble David, because David knew that God was a helper to those in distress and a refuge to all those who call on Him. And to all this, David found all the reason in the world to worship Him.

This was David's testimony about God. Ours may be a little different, but my goal is that you, too, would understand how great God is in your own life.

11

ASAPH, THE MUSICIAN

There are some names that do not need an introduction; if I were to mention Beethoven or Mozart, you likely would be familiar with the names and have probably heard one or two of their works. The same was very true for Asaph; he was a very talented musician. Everyone during the reign of David and for many years after knew well the name of Asaph. The average person today is not too privy to the life of Asaph. For that reason, I will begin with a brief introduction.

Asaph was of the tribe of Levi and one of a few men chosen by David to lead the music and choir in the tabernacle (1 Chron 6:31–32, 39). Some of the duties of Asaph are described in 1 Chronicles 16 and include ministering before the ark of the covenant daily. As was expected of a musician, Asaph wrote a few psalms. Psalms that are commonly attributed to Asaph are 50 and 73–83; we gather this because his name appears in the superscriptions. The psalms of Asaph were highly regarded; as we read from 2 Chronicles 29:30, Hezekiah, who reigned some 200 years after, ordered the Levites to praise the Lord with the words of David *and* Asaph. It is a reasonable high measure to have your psalm listed parallel to that of David.

Asaph was talented, regarded as a godly man, and trusted to lead the worship in the temple. In this chapter, we are going to look at Psalm 77, which is a psalm that is said to be written by Asaph. The goal as before is to see what this song-writer thought about God. As we walk through this psalm section at a time, we will see the magnitude of the Almighty God from the pen of Asaph. And perhaps we might adopt some of the thoughts that we too would see the magnitude of God displayed in our own lives.

Psalm 77

> I cried out to God for help; I cried out to God to hear me. When I was in distress, I sought the Lord; at night I stretched out untiring hands, and I would not be comforted (Ps 77:1–2).

I don't think it is a coincidence that this psalm began with a time of trouble. As much as I would love to say that God is glorified in our good times, we know that is not always the case. Sadly, our good times are not the most when we lean on God and watch Him work. But in our dark times, when we have no other place to turn, that is when we really see God move. That is when we are often reminded of His greatness.

When I first read this, I was reminded that Asaph was a musician, and so the question arose, is this a real story, or is it just a song? After all, consider many songs you might hear on the radio today; most of them are lavished with fictitious details to satisfy our musical appetites. However, I believe this psalm by Asaph was much more than that. I think this psalm, like all of David's, was penned from his heart, his personal experience, and his dark moment. In this particularly dark time of Asaph, he cried out to God in his trouble. The following verses help us to see into the heart of Asaph, and realize that even in his hardship, he *remembered* that his God was great.

> I remembered you, God, and I groaned; I meditated, and my spirit grew faint. You kept my eyes from closing; I was too troubled to speak. I thought about the former days, the years of long ago; I remembered my songs in the night. My heart meditated and my spirit asked: "Will the Lord reject forever? Will He never show His favor again? Has His unfailing love vanished forever? Has His promise failed for all time? Has God forgotten to be merciful? Has He in anger withheld His compassion" (Ps 77:3–9)?

Asaph remembered. This is a key thought in this psalm as we are going to see soon. What did he remember? Asaph remembered God; he remembered the psalms he wrote in past times. But Asaph would not be pulled out of this pit easily; this was are very dark place. He was so troubled that he couldn't even speak, so his prayer is full of groans to the Lord. And although his intellect is *remembering* his past psalms, his spirit is quite defeated and questioning if God really cares and is going to help this time. The text says that he meditated, but his spirit grew faint, then it pauses with a *selah*. A selah is believed to be a musical term to indicate a pause, perhaps to think, or ponder what was written. I think in the context, Asaph was putting emphasis on the struggle in his spirit. It seems that he wrote this, and afterward, he paused and put his head down, thought inside his heart, *God, I feel defeated.* There is a struggle within Asaph that I believe many of us can relate to. And that is okay; life is full of many struggles, and this just happens to be one of them. But what we will find most encouraging is to see what Asaph decided to do in this struggle of his:

> Then I thought, "To this I will appeal: the years when the Most High stretched out his right hand. I will remember the deeds of the Lord; yes, I will remember your miracles of long ago. I will consider all your works and meditate on all your mighty deeds" (Ps 77:10–12).

The beginning of this passage is rather complicated as you might see evident in the various ways different Bible translations handle it. Because of my lack of knowledge of the Hebrew text, I am going to follow the NIV. Looking at the context in the previous passage, we learned that Asaph was struggling within himself. He was remembering God and the past psalms he wrote to God, but his spirit was fighting against him as he had many doubts and fears. Asaph had to decide how he would respond.

In this passage, we learn that Asaph chose to trust in what he knew about God. He trusted in the deeds of God. He remembered and trusted in the miracles of God. He considered all the works of God and chose to continue to meditate on them. I want to return again to this idea that his spirit was feeling defeated and starting to consider the lies of the enemy. We too will find ourselves in those times where defeat seems like our companion. In those times, the enemy will throw at us whatever lie he can to help us forget. But like Asaph, we must resolve—*I will remember what God has done.*

What did Asaph remember? He continued the chapter by telling us:

> Your ways, God, are holy. What god is as great as our God? You are the God who performs miracles; you display your power among the peoples. With your mighty arm you redeemed your people, the descendants of Jacob and Joseph. The waters saw you, God, the waters saw you and writhed; the very depths were convulsed. The clouds poured down water, the heavens resounded with thunder; your arrows flashed back and forth. Your thunder was heard in the whirlwind, your lightning lit up the world; the earth trembled and quaked. Your path led through the sea, your way through the mighty waters, though your footprints were not seen. You led your people like a flock by the hand of Moses and Aaron (Ps 77:13–20).

What god is as great as our God? That pretty much sums it up. *God, there is no one who compares with You.* Asaph envisioned God to be so great that the waters were moved by the sight of God. He went on to say that the clouds even respond to the presence of God. Later in the passage, he spoke of thunder and lightning and said that it belongs to God. How powerful does someone have to be to possess thunder and lightning? Asaph had such a high view of God that he had no problem saying, *God, the thunder, the lightning, as unpredictable and untamable they may seem, I know they belong to You.* Finally, Asaph attributes the paths of the seas to the paths and footprints of God.

Asaph evidently was going through a difficult time in life, but he recalled the knowledge of God. Furthermore, not just knowledge, but a realization of how mighty God was and is. It was to these truths that Asaph was appealing. He was reasoning that if God is so great and has done so many amazing miracles, it is not out of His reach to help now.

Asaph closed this psalm by writing, "You led your people like a flock by the hand of Moses and Aaron" (Ps 77:20). Keeping in mind, Asaph just finished building up the case of the magnitude of God and that there is none who is like Him. He concluded by saying, *it was that same God that took care of His people during the time of Moses.* I think Asaph took that very truth to apply to the beginning of the psalm. Asaph was crying out to God, but his spirit was weak. I think what we see is the beginning-to-end struggle of Asaph; he was struggling, but the conclusion he came to was that God is powerful and incomparable. He has always taken care of His people as a shepherd. Therefore, the conclusion is that God would help Asaph.

JOB, A MAN HAVING GONE THROUGH THE FIRE

Many of us know the story of Job, at least the basics; he lost all he had in a matter of a day, had a tough and sometimes heated discussion with his companions, and ultimately, in the end, received a greater portion than before. But I would like to hone in on a particular chapter where we will see the testimony of Job concerning God. How a people think about God in their different stages of life speaks of their character. In the chapters of the book of Job, Job is stripped of all the luxuries that could have given him a *God is good because He has blessed me* attitude. What we are exposed to in the book of Job is the real, raw, and uncut version of a man in the fire. What Job says about God in those times will help us to see God in a very real way.

The passage of interest is Job 9:1–19. But before we go there, we need to look at how Job got there. In the very first chapter, the whole plot is set; Job loses everything he has. In chapter two, Job's friends showed up to help him in his time of need. They really did have sincere hearts. Starting in

chapter three and going through chapter thirty-seven, Job
and his friends went back and forth on *why* all the turmoil
was happening. Jobs friends presented the most logical
reason: *Job, you must have sinned.* After all, that was a very
common ideology in the Old Testament; God blesses the
righteous, and turmoil comes upon the sinners. That same
way of thinking was also seen during the time of Jesus; in
John nine, a man is brought to Jesus who had been born
blind. The first thing the disciples asked was who it was that
had sinned. They presumed it must had been for the sin of
the man born blind, or perhaps his parents. They would soon
realize that God was doing something for His glory. In the
story of Job, the friends quickly presumed sin must have
been the cause. They would all find out, but in the end, it is
not always that simple.

Job contended that he had done nothing that would
deserve such a judgment. But his friends continued to insist
that he obviously did something to upset God, and if nothing
else, perhaps he was being punished for his own pride. The
discussion turned heated at times, they went back and forth,
and ultimately they got nowhere and the scene was interrupted with God Himself speaking to Job.

How did we get to this point? Bildad, one of Job's friends,
just finished giving Job another rendition of the same
message: *Job, these kinds of bad things don't happen to people
unless they sinned. Job, what did you do?* It is in Job's response
that we learn a few remarkable things about God:

> Then Job replied: "Indeed, I know that this is true. But how
> can mere mortals prove their innocence before
> God? Though they wished to dispute with him, they could
> not answer him one time out of a thousand. His wisdom is
> profound, his power is vast. Who has resisted him and come

out unscathed? He moves mountains without their knowing it and overturns them in his anger. He shakes the earth from its place and makes its pillars tremble. He speaks to the sun and it does not shine; he seals off the light of the stars. He alone stretches out the heavens and treads on the waves of the sea. He is the Maker of the Bear and Orion, the Pleiades and the constellations of the south. He performs wonders that cannot be fathomed, miracles that cannot be counted. When he passes me, I cannot see him; when he goes by, I cannot perceive him. If he snatches away, who can stop him? Who can say to him, 'What are you doing?' God does not restrain his anger; even the cohorts of Rahab cowered at His feet. "How then can I dispute with him? How can I find words to argue with him? Though I were innocent, I could not answer him; I could only plead with my Judge for mercy. Even if I summoned him and he responded, I do not believe he would give me a hearing. He would crush me with a storm and multiply my wounds for no reason. He would not let me catch my breath but would overwhelm me with misery. If it is a matter of strength, he is mighty! And if it is a matter of justice, who can challenge him (Job 9:1–19)?

Immediately, I begin to realize that Job understood that there was quite a distinction and distance between himself and God. Even though Job thought for sure he had done nothing wrong, his response was, *I am only a man, I can't exactly go plead my case to God.* Furthermore, he argued that even if he could get the words to God's ears, why would He even take time to answer. It is not that Job thought he was worthless; he had such a large view of God. So large that he was left feeling that such a mighty God has no time to deal with little issues like his.

What fascinates me all the more is what Job said about what might happen if God *does* answer him. If a mere human speaks to any of us, they can use different volumes, tones, and so on. But all in all, there is nothing to fear. But Job had such a large view of God that he actually feared the idea of God responding; Job feared that if God did in fact respond, it would likely be the end of his life. Job explained himself in the verses provided above: God moves mountains, He speaks to the sun and it does not shine, He is the maker of constellations, He performs miracles that cannot be fathomed, we cannot see Him, and His anger is much to be feared. I only gave a quick overview of what Job thought, but it is evident that he did not look at God casually, but with the utmost respect and fear. What would happen if a God of such power comes into your presence to answer you? Job responded to that question.

If you were to ask Job what would happen if God were to respond to his concern, the answer would be simple. First Job would reiterate the situation: *You need to understand what we are talking about first. You have a complaint, or concern at best, that you want to take before God; not a mere man, but God. The Creator of the universe, the One who breathed life into all that breathes. The holy and unmatched God.* And after Job helps clarify what is being asked, his response would be simple and concise: *you would be crushed by a storm, and that storm would be God.*

Job imagined God's presence coming in as the fierceness of a storm that has the power to destroy the natural elements around. He was right to imagine such an image of God. In fact, when God answered Job in chapter thirty-eight, Job was told to brace himself like a man. Why did God give this command? I may be reading a little too far into the text, but I think I know why; God actually did come like a storm just as

Job expected. God came with a fierce and mighty storm so powerful that He had to warn Job, "Job, you better hang on tight." And I can just imagine that when God began speaking to Job, the natural elements around Job were crashing and being ripped apart as they could not contain the power of the Almighty. But out of mercy, Job was told to brace himself so that he might survive.

Job understood accurately the power of God. But as you can see if you read further into Job 38–42, what Job underestimated was the love and mercy of God. When God appeared to Job, He did come as a storm and could have crushed Job with ease. But God did not want to harm or punish Job; He wanted to see Job grow in his experience. Job learned so much about God from that experience, not only His might but also His character. Job had a fresh glimpse of the magnitude of God.

13

THE TESTIMONY GIVEN BY THE PHILISTINES

Paul spoke toward the lifelessness of idols in 1 Corinthians when he wrote, "an idol is nothing at all in the world" (1 Cor 8:4). Now of course, many people have always worshipped idols, believing they had some supernatural power to help or even heal. But one thing I think idol worshippers would agree on is that their idol remains where they put it. It's one thing to worship it for any odd reason, but it is another thing, and an undoubtable truth, that the idol is inanimate and cannot move itself nor does it have any physical power to harm a rival idol. I understand that this may not be the consensus for all idols, but I presume it may be safe to say it applies to the majority. I say all this to move toward a point. The story we will be looking at in this chapter is the time when the Philistines captured the ark of the covenant. We need to lay the ground work here. As we are going to see in the following text, the Philistines idol god was Dagon. I think it might be safe to say that everyone in Ashdod knew that Dagon did not move, could not take steps, could not speak, and definitely could not physically assault a rival idol. Nonetheless, Dagon was their god.

I think, to better understand the story, we might imagine Dagon not being a "god" as we understand our God in heaven, but more as a symbol or an icon. They offered worship to it and paid homage, but at the end of the day, they understood that Dagon was a cement statue that they formed with their bare hands a short time back. I say this because it gives us a better perspective on what was happening in Israel and Philistia in those days. When the Philistines captured the ark, they had no intentions of taking Israel's *God* into their camp. They had no intention of putting *god* against *god*. They were stealing what they thought to be Israel's icon, the symbol of home and unity. Steal the symbol and defeat their spirits, the flesh will fall shortly behind. That was their intention. So, they stole the ark and took it into their place of worship and placed it next to their icon—Dagon. Nothing was supposed to happen. In their view, it was a cement statue standing next to a wooden box. It wouldn't be long till they realized the ark was more than an icon. It wouldn't be long until they experienced the power of the One who sat on the seat between the cherubim. They would soon experience, in a horrific way, the magnitude of the one true God.

For the full story, you have to begin reading in 1 Samuel four, but to keep it a little shorter, for now, I am beginning in chapter five:

> After the Philistines had captured the ark of God, they took it from Ebenezer to Ashdod. Then they carried the ark into Dagon's temple and set it beside Dagon. When the people of Ashdod rose early the next day, there was Dagon, fallen on his face on the ground before the ark of the Lord! They took Dagon and put him back in his place. But the following

morning when they rose, there was Dagon, fallen on his face on the ground before the ark of the Lord! His head and hands had been broken off and were lying on the threshold; only his body remained. That is why to this day neither the priests of Dagon nor any others who enter Dagon's temple at Ashdod step on the threshold.

The Lord's hand was heavy on the people of Ashdod and its vicinity; He brought devastation on them and afflicted them with tumors. When the people of Ashdod saw what was happening, they said, "The ark of the god of Israel must not stay here with us, because His hand is heavy on us and on Dagon our god." So they called together all the rulers of the Philistines and asked them, "What shall we do with the ark of the god of Israel?"

They answered, "Have the ark of the god of Israel moved to Gath." So they moved the ark of the god of Israel.

But after they had moved it, the Lord's hand was against that city, throwing it into a great panic. He afflicted the people of the city, both young and old, with an outbreak of tumors. So they sent the ark of God to Ekron.

As the ark of God was entering Ekron, the people of Ekron cried out, "They have brought the ark of the God of Israel around to us to kill us and our people." So they called together all the rulers of the Philistines and said, "Send the ark of the God of Israel away; let it go back to its own place, or it will kill us and our people." For death had filled the city with panic; God's hand was very heavy on it. Those who did not die were afflicted with tumors, and the outcry of the city went up to heaven.

When the ark of the Lord had been in Philistine territory seven months, the Philistines called for the priests and the diviners and said, "What shall we do with the ark of the Lord? Tell us how we should send it back to its place."

They answered, "If you return the ark of the God of Israel, do not send it back to Him without a gift; by all means send a guilt offering to Him. Then you will be healed, and you will know why His hand has not been lifted from you."

The Philistines asked, "What guilt offering should we send to Him?"

They replied, "Five gold tumors and five gold rats, according to the number of the Philistine rulers, because the same plague has struck both you and your rulers. Make models of the tumors and of the rats that are destroying the country, and give glory to Israel's God. Perhaps He will lift His hand from you and your gods and your land. Why do you harden your hearts as the Egyptians and Pharaoh did? When Israel's god dealt harshly with them, did they not send the Israelites out so they could go on their way?

"Now then, get a new cart ready, with two cows that have calved and have never been yoked. Hitch the cows to the cart, but take their calves away and pen them up. Take the ark of the Lord and put it on the cart, and in a chest beside it put the gold objects you are sending back to him as a guilt offering. Send it on its way, but keep watching it. If it goes up to its own territory, toward Beth Shemesh, then the Lord has brought this great disaster on us. But if it does not, then we will know that it was not His hand that struck us but that it happened to us by chance."

So they did this. They took two such cows and hitched them to the cart and penned up their calves. They placed the ark of the Lord on the cart and along with it the chest containing the gold rats and the models of the tumors. Then the cows went straight up toward Beth Shemesh, keeping on the road and lowing all the way; they did not turn to the right or to the left. The rulers of the Philistines followed them as far as the border of Beth Shemesh.

I wonder what was going through the minds of the philistines when they woke up the first day and found Dagon fallen. I have a suspicion that, although they were filled curiosity, they weren't about to get suspicious—not yet at least. I mean, the list was endless of the reasons why Dagon was fallen over. Probably some juvenile needed a little discipline. But the next morning, their god was fallen *again*, but this time, his head and hands were broken off and lying on the threshold. That was when their superstition began; it says the men who came into the temple from that day forward were careful not to step on the threshold. They were not quite sure what was going on, but it made sense to them to keep away from that threshold. Time passed by, and they realized that many in the city were being afflicted with tumors. I am impressed that they so quickly connected these two events, and for their sake, they quickly realized that Dagon falling over and the tumors on the people were a result of them having the ark of the covenant in the camp. Their response was, "The ark of the God of Israel must not stay here with us, because His hand is heavy on us and on Dagon our god." So, they sent it away.

I question their rationale at this point that nether hey realized that the ark possessed a horrific power that they, nor their god Dagon, could harness. *So they sent it to their neighboring Philistine city!* When the ark arrived in Gath, it was not too long before the tumors began to afflict the people of that city as well. They didn't quite get the point, because they attempted to send the ark to yet another Philistine city, Ekron. However, the people of Ekron had been paying attention and realized that the ark was much more than a box overlayed with gold. Out of terror, they all agreed that the ark had to be returned to Israel.

I don't know if this is a digression from the point, but I have always been impressed at the respect the Philistines had gained for the ark of the covenant. They came to know of its power, and they even had a fresh glimpse of the power of the God of Israel. They were terrified and did not know what to do with it. In their best efforts, they wanted to get it out of the camp. As we saw in the text, they hoped that if they returned the ark, the God of Israel will lift His hand from them, from their gods, and from their land.

If Israel had as much respect as the Philistines had gained, the stories we read about them would have been much different. I am not saying we are any better, maybe you are, maybe you are not. I think we all have a tendency to diminish the power of God in our minds. He in fact had never changed from being that Almighty Divine who spoke creation into existence, but in our minds, we sometimes feel we can argue with Him or blame Him for our troubles. We sometimes feel that He does not, and therefore cannot, do miracles anymore. There really is no wonder why many don't pray. As our view of God diminishes, so do our prayers; after all, why pray to a God who is not strong and mighty? The God of creation was mighty, the God who parted the Red Sea was mighty, and the God who sat upon the ark was mighty, *but not our God*. I think the adversary has gotten to many of us and the product is that don't see God for who He is.

The Philistines were a pagan nation. They had set up their own idols to worship. But during the days in the text above, they would experience God in a way that many of us need to.

PART 4: THE GOD OF REVERENT AWE

In the book of Revelation, John was in the Spirit when he was taken up into heaven and saw some remarkable things. Stopping just for a moment, I know the previous phrase can stir some compelling arguments. But for the sake of my point in this chapter, what is important is what John *saw* and *heard*. In chapter four of Revelation, John was found standing before the throne of God. It is a fascinating sight. He saw the throne and the One sitting on the throne. He saw the twenty-four elders surrounding the throne. There was thunder and lightning flashing all around. He saw the seven spirits of the God before the throne. Nearer to the throne, John saw four living creatures whose descriptions are quite fascinating and perhaps unimaginable. Those living creatures were speaking from the heavens a tone that John would write for all generations after him to read:

"Holy, holy, holy
    is the Lord God Almighty,

who was, and is, and is to come" (Rev 4:8b).

The word "holy" comes from the Latin, *sanctus.* Many know that word in its various forms such as *sanctuary* or *sanctum.* This word used in the New Testament is *sanctify* or sanctification. These all have one meaning that will be the theme of this chapter—separateness. In the following chapters, we will be specifically looking at that quality of God's *holiness* that would merit *reverent awe.* Let's be honest, just because something is separate does not mean it is reverent or full of awe. However, God is holy—separate. And in these next chapters, we will notice that in many facets of God's separateness, He is just that.

14

THE FEAR OF THE LORD

That day when evening came, he said to his disciples, "Let us go over to the other side." Leaving the crowd behind, they took him along, just as he was, in the boat. There were also other boats with him. A furious squall came up, and the waves broke over the boat, so that it was nearly swamped. Jesus was in the stern, sleeping on a cushion. The disciples woke him and said to him, "Teacher, don't you care if we drown?"

He got up, rebuked the wind and said to the waves, "Quiet! Be still!" Then the wind died down and it was completely calm.

He said to His disciples, "Why are you so afraid? Do you still have no faith?"

They were terrified and asked each other, "Who is this? Even the wind and the waves obey him" (Mark 4:35–41)!

The disciples watched Jesus preach, they witnessed Him forgive sins, and they even saw Him heal the lame. They thought they had Him all figured out. He was everything they expected the coming Messiah to be. But this night would break the walls of the box they had put Jesus in. They woke Jesus up, but not to command the storm, but to bale water. *Grab a bucket and pull your weight.* I don't mean to sound rude, but when you are on the precipice of sure death, it seems sensible that your Master should help as well. So they woke Jesus; Peter was probably holding a bucket to hand Jesus. They watched as Jesus stood up, but He did not help bale water. He stood up and spoke three simple words; "Quiet, Be still!" Do you know how our minds can process a phrase before it is even spoken? We can have a whole response played out in just a mere split second. I wonder about the split second upon Jesus saying those three words. What was the disciple's response? In that split second, I have to believe the disciples were astonished at what they had just heard. At first though, not out of positive amazement, but perhaps hopeless unbelief. Face it, what would you be thinking if you were in Peter's shoes? People can't just command storms; it just doesn't happen! The math is simple: water—buckets—bale—or die. But while that moment was testing the faith of the disciples, the unimaginable happened. As soon as Jesus uttered the last word, the storm stopped. The storm was not the only thing that stood still at that moment. They all stood there in awe and were not exactly sure how to process the reality of what three words from the mouth of Jesus could do. I mean, they knew He could preach —but this? Even forgiving sins and healing a leg was acceptable—but to command a storm? To have words penetrate into the heavens and produce change—only God has done that in creation. It was at that moment they realized what just happen, and they were terrified. They were learning to fear Jesus; they were learning the fear of the Lord.

What is the fear of the Lord? As a preface, I will admit that this topic is way too big for me, and I am far from fully comprehending it myself. But I will give you the best biblical answer I have. Furthermore, this answer is by no means an exhaustive response, but just a simple overview. The fear of the Lord is the realization that we will stand and give an account for our sins one day before an Almighty God. He is going to pick up his Word by which He will judge us, and we will be judged accordingly. If we live in Christ, we are covered by His blood. However, if we are living in sin, all we should have is a fearful expectation of damnation (Heb 10:26–27). We serve a loving and forgiving God, but He is also a God who cannot stand before sin; it is against His very nature. And as we serve a God who is true to His Word and will reward our faithfulness, the same is true of His Word; those who live in sin will *not* receive that reward.

The fear of the Lord is the beginning of knowledge (Prov 1:7), and also the beginning of wisdom (Prov 9:10, Ps 111:10). By today's measure, a person might be deemed wise or knowledgeable by a few different standards. The Scriptures say the beginning, the very first essence of wisdom is the fear of the Lord. Therefore, if a person were to pursue wisdom or knowledge, the beginning of that journey is such fear; without it, the journey is halted. Furthermore, not only is the fear of the Lord the beginning, but it teaches wisdom as well (Prov 13:33). Jeremiah wrote that the fear of the Lord is not only for our good but for the good of our children (Jer 32:39). The fear of the Lord is a treasure of ever-increasing value.

The fear of the Lord is rooted in having a fresh revelation

and realization of God. The following Scriptures are just a handful of the plethora of evidence to prove this point:

- After Israel watched God pour out judgment on the Egyptians, Exodus 14:31 says they *feared* God.
- God parted the Red Sea and the Jordan by which Joshua later told Israel that God did so that they would fear Him (Josh 4:23–24).
- During the days of King Jehoshaphat, when the surrounding kingdoms realized that Israel's God was fighting for them, they feared Him (2 Chron 20:29).
- When Ananias and Sapphira fell dead after lying to the apostles, the people feared the Lord (Acts 5).
- Jesus himself told the disciples, "Do not be afraid of those who kill the body but cannot kill the soul. Rather, be afraid of the one who can destroy both soul and body in hell (Matt 10:28).
- And finally, and also one of my favorite stories, when Jesus calmed the storm, His disciples feared God (Mark 4:35–41).

The fear of the Lord is rooted in having an understanding of who God is. The problem that often arises is that we personally never saw God part a sea or calm a storm. And because of that, some may not fear God appropriately. But if we search the Scriptures and get to know God and understand that He is the *same* God from creation till now, we will understand the profound fact; He should be feared today as He was feared those many years ago, for He has never changed.

The fear of the Lord keeps a person from sin. Proverbs 8:13 says, "To fear the Lord is to hate evil; I hate pride and arrogance, evil behavior and perverse speech." It is impossible to willfully live in sin and possess the fear of the Lord; they oppose one another. Moses told the people that they were tested in order that they would learn to fear the Lord. The purpose he says is that it would keep them from sinning (Exod 20:20). Leviticus 19:14 and 25:17 both warn the people not to live in particular sins, but rather fear the Lord. Malachi gives a list of sins and says that those who practice them are those who do not fear the Lord. Again, living in sin and possessing the fear of the Lord were thought to be two completely different lifestyles. If you willfully sin, Scripture says you do not fear God. Furthermore, Scripture says that if you learn the fear of the Lord, it will teach you not to sin. Solomon said, "The fear of the Lord is a fountain of life, turning a person from the snares of death" (Prov 14:27). It is the fear of God that causes a person to run from sin. Jeremiah said the same thing but worded just a bit different; "I will inspire them to fear me, so that they will never turn away from me" (Jer 32:40). That really is what living an upright and Godly life comes down to; fearing God. If we are honest with ourselves, I think we will all agree that none of us have the unction to live upright in and of ourselves. There must be something in us that when we think of the Almighty God, we have a fearful desire to live in a way that pleases Him.

David wrote this concerning the fear of the Lord,

Who, then, are those who fear the Lord? He will instruct them in the ways they should choose. They will spend their days in prosperity, and their descendants will inherit the land. The Lord confides in those who fear him; he makes his covenant known to them (Ps 25:12–14).

I think it should be a desire of everyone to grow in the fear of the lord. When the disciples were in the boat with Jesus, as we saw in the introduction of this chapter, they learned the fear of the Lord. They learned as they were given a fresh revelation of Jesus—God. But the fear of the Lord is not merely an attitude of being, but a motion. As it was also for the disciple, the fear of the Lord will compel us to follow after God. But also remembering what we read earlier, it is only the *beginning* of wisdom and knowledge. The fear of the Lord is only the beginning of the journey. When you embark from there, the Lord will continue to instruct you and do amazing things in your life.

15

THE DAY OF THE LORD

There have been days that have stood apart from all other days and have impacted history in the most profound ways. These days are often recorded, remembered, sometimes rejoiced, and sometimes mourned. One of those days in history and what has impacted the whole world is what has been called "D–Day." D–Day was that dreadful yet wonderful time on June 6, 1944, when allied forces of the United States, the United Kingdom, Canada, and many more stormed the beaches of Normandy and ultimately changed the course of the second world war. It was a tremendous force of about 150,000 soldiers storming the German forces by land, sea, and air. It was a day of victory, but it did not go without losses; about 4,414 lives of the allied forces were mourned that day. It was a day that the world will never forget.

This chapter is not about one particular day, but a "day" that would come to represent any day of great disaster when judgment was issued from God. There are such days seen in the Old Testament as well as the New. These days have been called "the day of the Lord." But what was such a day? In this chapter, I am going to unveil many of the occasions of the day of the Lord in the Bible. This is going to build a case that will aid in helping us understand what such a day was by the end of the chapter. But I urge you not to get lost in the textual detail, the purpose of this entire book is the unveil the greatness of God. So, while we are studying stories that have a fascinating narrative of disaster, earthquakes, the moon turning to blood, and the sun darkening, we must not be distracted from the point; the reader of these stories is intended to stand in awe of the God who has such power to do the things we are about to see.

God spoke clearly through his prophet Zephaniah concerning the day of the Lord. The prophecy of Zephaniah was ultimately to the whole world who were being called to repentance. With the plea to repent, God also brought a warning that if they did not, they would see destruction. The entire three-chapter book should be read for context, but for sake of space, I will only quote a few verses:

Be silent before the Sovereign Lord, for the day of the Lord is near. The Lord has prepared a sacrifice; He has consecrated those He has invited. "On the day of the Lord's sacrifice I will punish the officials and the king's sons and all those clad in foreign clothes. On that day I will punish all who avoid stepping on the threshold, who fill the temple of their gods with violence and deceit. "On that day," declares the Lord, "a cry will go up from the Fish Gate, wailing from the New Quarter, and a loud crash from the hills. Wail, you who live in the market district; all your merchants will be wiped out, all who trade with silver will be destroyed. At that time I will search Jerusalem with lamps and punish those who are complacent, who are like wine left on its dregs, who think, "The Lord will do nothing, either good or bad." Their wealth will be plundered, their houses demolished. Though they build houses, they will not live in them; though they plant vineyards, they will not drink the wine." The great day of the Lord is near—near and coming quickly. The cry on the day of the Lord is bitter; the Mighty Warrior shouts His battle cry. That day will be a day of wrath—a day of distress and anguish, a day of trouble and ruin, a day of darkness and gloom, a day of clouds and blackness—a day of trumpet and battle cry against the fortified cities and against the corner towers. "I will bring such distress on all people that they will grope about like those who are blind, because they have sinned against the Lord. Their blood will be poured out like dust and their entrails like dung. Neither their silver nor their gold will be able to save them on the day of the Lord's wrath." In the fire of His jealousy the whole earth will be consumed, for He will make a sudden end of all who live on the earth (Zeph 1:7–18).

We do not have to read far to realize that that *day* was unlike any usual day. On that day, God said He was going to sweep everything from the face of the earth, from all creatures on earth to the birds in the sky and the fish in the sea. He later said in the same chapter that the whole earth would be consumed by the fire of His jealousy. In a blink of an eye, all that was would be no more. Furthermore, God said that day would come *near*. Commentators have a wide range of ideas on how to reconcile these verses. An honest eye would admit that this sounds a lot like the end of mankind. But was it? God said it would be near, but that was about 2,600 years ago. At the same time, we cannot dismiss it; it is Scripture. However, we do need this passage and the many others like it to make sense. In this case, to help us understand, I think we need to start at the end—Revelation.

In the book of Revelation, John introduced what many call the "Day of the Lord," and for good reason. In chapter six, we see the four horsemen who represent the evil that had been plaguing the world. Evil had permeated the whole known world until we get to the fifth seal where God's people called out asking God, "how long?" When we see the sixth seal opened, it is a picture of God responding:

> I watched as he opened the sixth seal. There was a great earthquake. The sun turned black like sackcloth made of goat hair, the whole moon turned blood red, and the stars in the sky fell to earth, as figs drop from a fig tree when shaken by a strong wind. The heavens receded like a scroll being rolled up, and every mountain and island was removed from its place.
>
> Then the kings of the earth, the princes, the generals, the rich, the mighty, and everyone else, both slave and free, hid in caves and among the rocks of the mountains. They called to the mountains and the rocks, "Fall on us and hide us from the face of him who sits on the throne and from the wrath of the Lamb! For the great day of their wrath has come, and who can withstand it" (Rev 6:12–17)?

I understand that there are many things in the book of Revelation that can be debated till *the cows come home*. But when looking at this passage, I hope we all can see and agree on one thing; there are some strange and terrible things that John said would happen: first, there were earthquakes on this day of the Lord. Then, but not to assume a sequential order but a culmination of events, the sun was darkened. Then the moon was turned to blood, and the stars fell to the earth. It is no wonder many have interpreted the book of Revelation to be the end of days. After all, John himself writes at the end of the passage, "Who can withstand it?" The assumption would be *no one*, it's the end of mankind. But that is not what the text reveals. If you read through and ignore the chapter break, you will see that the righteous will indeed survive such a dreadful day of the Lord. These verses may not be speaking of the end of the world. But if not, what are they speaking of?

The phenomenal events listed in Revelation six are actually taken from Old Testament Scripture. And because of that, we are going to try to understand why and what this means.

- Isaiah 13:9–10 speaks of the day of the Lord when the stars, constellations, and the moon will not give light.
- Isaiah 34:4 speaks of how the stars will fall.
- Jeremiah 4:23–24 and 28 speak of the heavenly lights not giving their light, and also earthquakes.
- Joel 2:10 speaks of earthquakes, and the sun and moon darkened.
- Joel 2:30–31 speaks of the sun turning dark and the moon turning to blood.
- Amos 8:9 speaks of the sun and moon darkened.

After seeing these verses, perhaps your initial idea of Revelation changed if your first thought those events were intended to end the world. Because as history has shown us, in each of the passages quoted in the book of Revelation, they spoke of the day of the Lord, but not the end of the world. In each of the passages, it was not pending events of the end-times, but the text that speaks of the day of the Lord ushers in judgment from God. Furthermore, we see histori-cally that these events were not to be interpreted literally but intended to give the people of God an image of what the fierce hand of God may look like as it punishes the wicked—not even nature itself can stand in the way.

Before I move on, I want to clarify a few more items in Revelation. Revelation has long been thought to be a book forecasting the last days. We do not have time to cover that topic in detail right now, but we have to be honest with a few things. Revelation six uses the same language as many Old Testament passages. However, in the Old Testament, we understand those verses to speak of punishment, and in a very *figurative* way. For some reason, many turn to Revela-tion six and take it literally and are waiting for a day when the sun will literally stop giving its light and turn to blood. I believe it may not be the most honest interpretation of the book; furthermore, Revelation six begins with horsemen. Notice how easy and necessary it is to read the first eleven verses figuratively. But then we get to verse twelve, when the sixth seal ushers in these events, many quickly label them as the end of the world. My proposal is that Revelation 6:12–17 is not the end of the world; it is a day of judgment. It is a day when the Lord will get up from His throne and with His power, He will penetrate the earth's atmosphere, but nature itself cannot contain God. It will be the day of the Lord.

I would like to try to bring this to a closing point. I think we quickly lose focus when we see these passages; we are so quick to see the forces of nature and picture what it would look like and if could it possibly be the end. But that's not the point. I believe when these passages were read to the people, God's motive was that He wanted the people to see *Him*—God, *their* God, who cannot even enter the atmosphere without nature being disrupted. We first see it during creation; a single word sent creativity through the universe. When Moses was on Mount Sinai, God met him there. Smoke covered the mountain, the mountain trembled, and there was lightning and thunder. Coincidence? No, nature could not handle such a close encounter with its creator. We see this time and time again. It is the same when God had to respond in anger. Such times when God had to say enough is enough, and not even the elements of nature could withstand such a force. The day of the Lord says something phenomenal about our God; He has a *day* that is labeled after Him; the *day of the Lord.* But we must not miss the point here. Whether it be because of God's judgment, His creation, or just Him speaking to Moses or Elijah, one thing is clear from these events; there is something fascinating about God that is so infinitely big and not even the sun in all of its vastness can stand before Him without melting.

PART 5: THE GOD OF GREATNESS

This part is one of my favorites. Herein, I do not discuss the quality of the power or fierceness of God or even His presence. In this part, I will show you the quality of God's *character*. For greatness is not only found in might and power, but also in the quality of one's essence.

If the greatness of God was only measured by the exertion of His power, He would still be great and unmatched, but also too easily rivaled by myths of other deities. It is not difficult to muster up a story of a deified being of power and might. Often in such stories, the author is careful to describe the importance of such a being, its power, its might, its fierceness—all the reasons it might need to usurp the worship of its followers. But there is something different found in God that I am not sure can be found in any other.

William Arthur Ward once said, "Greatness is not found in possessions, power, position, or prestige. It is discovered in goodness, humility, service, and character." This is precisely what we see in God and what will be explored in the following chapters. We have seen in the earlier chapters how even the voice of God can transform worlds. But in the following chapters, we are going to see how God allows Himself to *feel* the pain and hurt of His creation; we are going to look at the compassion of God. We have seen how even the presence of God disturbs the natural elements of the earth. We have seen how the very testimony of God has transformed lives. Lastly, we have seen how God is to be feared and respected with revenant awe. But out of all the stories of greatness we have read above, I believe the greatest act of God that reveals just how great He is will be seen in the final chapter entitled *The Selfless Power of the Almighty*. It has often been taken for granted, but the story of Jesus is the paramount example of the power of God. He is the creator of the universe. He existent before the foundations of the world. His power is unmatched and truly not even comprehendible. Yet, due to His heart of compassion and desire for justice, He demonstrates His greatest might through an act of love.

16

GOD AND HIS COMPASSION

Whatd do you think when you consider the story of Nineveh, more commonly known as Jonah and the whale? I think that might have been a distraction for many. The book is called Jonah, so you naturally keep a close eye on Jonah. He is swallowed by a big fish and spit up on dry ground three days later. So, we as readers naturally keep our attention on this big fish, often thought to be a whale. I am not sure there is a sermon out there that does not contain some aspect of the big fish. There are a few verses in the story about Nineveh, but then the narrative quickly shifts back to Jonah and his attitude about what God was doing. I am not saying there is anything wrong with that, but what I would like to do with this time is look carefully to see what we learn from or about God. And in this case it is right in the text; one single verse hidden in this four-chapter book. But what it says about God cannot even fit into the comprehension of the most imaginative person. Jonah knew; he didn't understand or like it, but he knew:

[Jonah] prayed to the Lord, "Isn't this what I said, Lord, when I was still at home? That is what I tried to forestall by fleeing to Tarshish. I knew that you are a gracious and compassionate God, slow to anger and abounding in love, a God who relents from sending calamity" (Jonah 4:2).

Jonah knew that God was a God of compassion. There was no other reason He would be extending an opportunity to repent to this undeserving city. Jonah had no interest in sharing this amazing gift with the wicked people of Nineveh. So, he literally got in a boat and went in the opposite direction. There are several things we can do at this point; we could look at Jonah and the big fish. We could look and Jonah and his attitude at the end. We could look at Jonah and his hatred for the Ninevites. Those would all make great studies, and often great sermons, but not they will not serve us in this chapter. What I would like to look at is *God and His compassion*. Because therein I believe we are going to catch a glimpse of the greatness of God that has impacted each of our lives more than we often know.

What is compassion? Some synonyms used are mercy, kindness, love, steadfast love, and, lovingkindness. I could go into Greek, but I think we all get the point. I am going to propose that from the verses given, perhaps the account within the book of Jonah is a story of God's compassion. Such an act is precisely what Jonah was afraid of. God has been known for many things over the ages, but when we look at Jonah, God was full of compassion.

Jonah hated the idea that God was so eager to show mercy to the people of Nineveh. Why? The makers of the children's series, *Veggie Tales*, gave us a humorous perspective in their movie called *Jonah*. In the movie that poetically follows the story in the Bible, Jonah did not want to go to the city of Nineveh, and he calls the people, "fish slappers." Now, we can all agree that there was no *fish slapping* in the Bible, as far as I can tell. But it is a way to show kids how mean and awful the people in the city were—fish slapping was wrong and hated by God; it was a *kid-friendly* image of sin. Apparently, the people in Nineveh (in the movie version) had an incessant desire to slap each other with fish. It was nonstop all day and night. For that, Jonah thought they were not worthy of any gift from God, especially mercy. But as the story goes on, Jonah ended up in Nineveh preaching to the "fish slappers" and exhorting them to repent.

Again, the people in Nineveh were not fish slappers, but they were a people full of sin; immoralities that we don't even want our kids knowing about till they're older. I think we all have thought like Jonah at some time; thinking that some people are just too evil to change or even deserve to change. That is exactly where Jonah was.

Jesus spoke of the same thing in Matthew 20:1–16, the parable of vineyard workers. Some have worked so hard and strived so long, perhaps their whole life to be righteous, to receive the eternal reward. And they know that one day they will. Those are the ones who started working early in the day. The difficulty arises when some workers came later in the day, those who found salvation later, perhaps after living a whole life of sin. And if they found Christ before they take that final breath, they were also promised that same eternal reward. I think Jonah thought of himself as one who had worked hard for righteousness' sake and took pride in calling himself a child of God. And to watch God pour out the *same* gifts on the wicked who did not even want it; well, to Jonah, that was downright unfair, and not even just. So much so that he was angry at God for such actions. But this isn't a story of fairness nor are we going to make this all about Jonah; it is a story of compassion, the compassion of God.

Another reason I think Jonah struggled was that he was a Hebrew. That meant he was one of God's chosen people, the children of promise. There was an ideology throughout the Old Testament and into the New that suggested that God's salvation was *only* for the Jewish people—the Hebrews. However, Paul argued against this all throughout his letter to the Romans. Paul clarified that the Jews were not children of God merely because they were sons of Isaac and had the law, but because they were sons of promise. The promise was given to Abraham many years *before* the law; the promise was for all humanity. It was hard for many to fully understand and accept this truth. It seems possible that Jonah was the one who struggled with this. He clearly understood that salvation was possible for even the pagans of Nineveh, but he didn't seem to think they deserved it. The theological truth to consider is that none of us deserve the compassion of God.

One day Moses petitioned God saying, "Show me your glory." A very interesting phrase; Moses had known God, but he wanted to know God more. Moses wanted God to reveal His true nature. God did just what Moses asked:

And the Lord said, "Here is a place by Me, and you shall stand on the rock. So it shall be, while My glory passes by, that I will put you in the cleft of the rock, and will cover you with My hand while I pass by. Then I will take away My hand, and you shall see My back; but My face shall not be seen." [for the sake of relevance, I am omitting 34:1-4]

Now the Lord descended in the cloud and stood with him there, and proclaimed the name of the Lord. And the Lord passed before him and proclaimed, "The Lord, the Lord God, merciful and gracious, longsuffering, and abounding in goodness and truth, keeping mercy for thousands, forgiving iniquity and transgression and sin, by no means clearing *the guilty,* visiting the iniquity of the fathers upon the children and the children's children to the third and the fourth generation." (Exod 33:21–23, 34:5–7 NKJV)

There are literally a thousand adjectives God could have used here to describe His glorified nature. He could have begun with the fancy ones we all know, *omnipotent, omniscient,* or *omnipresent.* He could have gone with the *Jehovah* names; *Jehovah Jireh, your provider* or *Jehovah Nissi, your banner,* or the many others we know. But He didn't. As wonderful as those names are and how well they describe God, that is not how He described His glory. God spoke, and these are the words that came out, "I am your God, your *compassionate* God" (paraphrased to make a point).

It says something about a person (or God) when you see what they want to be known for. God is known for many things. But in the case of Moses and I believe with us as well, God wanted to be known for His mercy, His kindness, love, steadfast love, and His lovingkindness, which are all aspects of compassion. I don't think there has ever been a god devised or created with such features as the one and only Christian God.

I want to wrap this chapter up by making it *real.* We all have heard many stories of people accusing God as a wrathful God. But I urge you to understand the balance here because it really is not balanced at all; *the scales are tips greatly in our favor.* God reserved wrath toward the sinners who refuse to repent. And that is as simple as it is; that is what God's wrath is reserved for. Solomon, in his wisdom, wrote, "Be sure of this: The wicked will not go unpunished, but those who are righteous will go free" (Prov 11:21). A few chapters later, he added, "If imposing a fine on the innocent is not good, surely to flog honest officials is not right" (Prov 17:26). The point I am making is that God only judges the wicked. With this, I want to bring our minds back to where we began:

> [Jonah] prayed to the Lord, "Isn't this what I said, Lord, when I was still at home? That is what I tried to forestall by fleeing to Tarshish. I knew that you are a gracious and compassionate God, slow to anger and abounding in love, a God who relents from sending calamity" (Jonah 4:2).

The compassion of God works in the favor of His creation, all of humanity. God extended His mercy toward the wicked begging them to repent. God exhausted all of His resources, even His own Son, to try to save every person from their own sin. God has never wanted calamity on anyone. If people experience the wrath of God, it is because they first refused over and over the good mercies and compassion of the One who wants to save them.

17

THE HOLY GOD

Have you recently taken time to consider what it means for God to be *holy*? The word literally means to be *set apart, distinct,* or *different.* God made a clear declaration to the nation when He was giving Israel their laws to guide their behavior, He said, "You are to be holy to me because I, the Lord, am holy, and I have set you apart from the nations to be my own" (Lev 20:26). Peter quoted this passage in his letter to the early church (1 Pet 1:16). This is a timeless truth and has depths to explore that go deeper than this book can dive. To get a nuance of what holiness means, and furthermore, to understand what God has in mind when He asks us to be holy, I think it appropriate to understand His holiness. This chapter is going to share an aspect about God and His holiness that I missed for so long. I am overjoyed to be able to write it now, and I pray that it speaks to your heart as richly as it has mine.

The idea that has pervaded theology for all of time is that God is in heaven as we are on earth. There are many images of grandeur seen throughout the Old Testament testifying to this perception. I always appreciated the words of Isaiah when he saw into heaven, he said,

> ... I saw the Lord, high and exalted, seated on a throne; and the train of his robe filled the temple. Above him were seraphim, each with six wings: With two wings they covered their faces, with two they covered their feet, and with two they were flying. And they were calling to one another: "Holy, holy, holy is the Lord Almighty; the whole earth is full of his glory" (Isa 6:1–3).

Jesus testified of this same truth when He was teaching the disciples how to pray; He told them, "This, then, is how you should pray: 'Our Father in heaven, hallowed be your name ... '" (Matt 6:9). God is on His throne and He is holy. I want to propose a question, but don't worry, I will continue to answer it in the next paragraph. See, we are separate from God right now, but one day, those who are in Christ will one day stand in heaven; we will be standing before the throne of God. My question then is: *if we will one day be standing before the throne of God, and He will be right there in front of us with no more firmament or curse of sin to separate us—will He still be holy?* Before you drop the book and call me a heretic, please keep reading.

I want to answer the question by reading a portion of Scripture that gives us a glimpse into the throne room of God. While taking a look inside, we will see something amazing:

> At once I was in the Spirit, and there before me was a throne in heaven with someone sitting on it. And the one who sat there had the appearance of jasper and ruby. A rainbow that shone like an emerald encircled the throne.

Surrounding the throne were twenty-four other thrones, and seated on them were twenty-four elders. They were dressed in white and had crowns of gold on their heads. From the throne came flashes of lightning, rumblings and peals of thunder. In front of the throne, seven lamps were blazing. These are the seven spirits of God. Also, in front of the throne there was what looked like a sea of glass, clear as crystal.

In the center, around the throne, were four living creatures, and they were covered with eyes, in front and in back. The first living creature was like a lion, the second was like an ox, the third had a face like a man, the fourth was like a flying eagle. Each of the four living creatures had six wings and was covered with eyes all around, even under its wings. Day and night they never stop saying: "Holy, holy, holy is the Lord God Almighty, who was, and is, and is to come" (Rev 4:2–8).

It was at the moment of reading this passage that I realized that the holiness of God is not rooted merely in His location; there is something more distinctive about God than the fact that we are on the earth and He is in heaven. When reading this passage, I noticed all those creatures, elders, and seemingly *all* of heaven. Some were round about the throne and within arm's reach. They understood. Something about God was *still* so separate from them being right next to His throne that they all bowed down day and night and cried out, "Holy, holy, holy." Again, when I stand before the throne of God, will he still be holy? Yes!

To imagine that God is only holy because He is on a distant throne is to miss so much of the fullness and magnitude of God. His very nature and virtue are equal to none other. There will be a day when I will stand before the

Almighty God. On that day, I will be in my glorified new body. I will be as perfect as I will ever be made. And while standing before the God of heaven, my Designer and Creator, I will fall down with all the rest of heaven, and I too will cry out, "Holy, holy, holy."

18

THE SELFLESS NATURE OF THE ALMIGHTY

W hat a person, *or Deity*, does when they possess power and control is telling of their character. And I have found this very facet of God to be fascinating. Consider for a moment the Greek gods. For the American culture today, the Greek gods are more or less folklore taught in schools or statues marveled at museums and art shows. I have not met anyone who believes in the existence of the Greek pantheon. Nonetheless, it makes a very intriguing English or history class. However, for the world around and before the time of Jesus, this was a prevalent religious system that many were quite devout to. We learn a lot about these gods when we take note of the common image of Olympus painted in history books and movies; the gods were always at war with one another, fighting for power and vengeance. Jealousy and envy were always prevalent. Their care for humanity was only a marginal concern; they were more often focused on their own interests. But we see quite a different pattern when considering the Jewish and Christian God found throughout the pages of the Bible. This chapter is going to reveal the unique quality of God that sets Him apart from all others. This chapter will unveil the selfless nature of the Almighty.

Did you notice how I deviated from the topic of power? The whole book has focused on the majesty and splendor of the one true God, and that majesty has often been demonstrated in different forms of power, but here we are going to look at the *selfless nature* of God. However, is it really a deviation from power, or is that just how we have learned to think in some ways? It is quick and easy to associate power with strength and valor; power is found in the voice of one who can utter creation into existence, and in the shaking of mountains and the parting of seas. But in a selfless action? For some that would be *powerless.* But I believe such an act is a perfect demonstration of power; after all, don't we sing the words; "there is power, power, power in the blood." Selfless acts are the most revered displays of power.

Or maybe we have it all wrong; maybe our *American* minds have gotten us distracted with power. What if God wants us to consider the character, and how the character can dictate our actions? Call it power or call it humility, I wonder if it matters at all; isn't it the same at the end of the day? Put all things aside, it comes down to one's character. And with all power to seize and all authority to control, God decides to act selflessly toward mankind. Many may think that profound; I find it mesmerizing.

I want to come back to Exodus 33 and 34 when Moses asked God to reveal His glory. In essence, Moses was saying, *God, I want to know You more.* This was God's response:

> The Lord, the Lord, the compassionate and gracious God, slow to anger, abounding in love and faithfulness, maintaining love to thousands, and forgiving wickedness, rebel-

lion and sin. Yet he does not leave the guilty unpunished; he punishes the children and their children for the sin of the parents to the third and fourth generation (Exod 34:6–7).

What God reveals about Himself in this passage is that He has a heart full of love that will do anything He can to show mercy and forgiveness to all people. And this is exactly what we continually see throughout the narrative of the Old Testament.

The Old Testament narrative has often been misunderstood to such a point that some have thought the God of the Old Testament is a different the God of the New. The former was a mean and hateful God full of wrath. The God of the New Covenant is a loving God who came with mercy. But this would stand contrary to God's declaration to Moses. I want to first contend that they are both the same God. I also contend that He, that one God, is a merciful and selflessly loving God, and has always been.

We already looked at the ark of the covenant in a previous chapter. However, we focused on the power; such power that a person could not touch it, nonetheless even look upon it. But if we look beyond the awe of the power, we see love and mercy:

You shall make a mercy seat of pure gold; two and a half cubits shall be its length and a cubit and a half its width. And you shall make two cherubim of gold; of hammered work you shall make them at the two ends of the mercy seat. Make one cherub at one end, and the other cherub at the other end; you shall make the cherubim at the two ends of it of one piece with the mercy seat. And the cherubim shall stretch out their wings above, covering the mercy seat with their wings, and they shall face one another; the faces of the cherubim shall be toward the mercy seat. You shall put the mercy seat on top of the ark, and in the ark you shall put the Testimony that I will give you. And there I will meet with you, and I will speak with you from above the mercy seat, from between the two cherubim which are on the ark of the Testimony, about everything which I will give you in commandment to the children of Israel (Exod 25:17–22 NKJV).

Let me try to simplify this. The mercy seat is also spoken of in Hebrews 9:5 and is called the *atonement cover* in some translations. The Greek word used is *hilasterion*, which means, "that which makes "expiation" or "propitiation." The mercy seat has always been associated with the removal of sin. God was raising up Israel to be His people, and He could have led them any way He wanted. After all, He is the God of the universe. In His power, He gave Moses the instructions to build the ark with a *mercy seat* upon. God wanted the people to have a place where they could have their sins atoned for. What was the selfless act of God? Although it was a temporary *shadow*, God created for the people a salvation— His mercy.

I see the mercy of God demonstrated by selfless acts all throughout the pages of the Old Testament. Reading through the Judges, there is an evident cycle that takes place: the leader of Israel dies; each person does as he pleases and the nation falls into sin; God sends a nation to punish them; the people cry out to God in repentance; God sends a deliverer. The same God that spoke to Moses many years prior was actively pursuing his people—selfless love. The same love is seen during the times of the kings; God would often send a nation to punish His people when they wandered from Him. Someone might call it vindictive—I call it selfless love; a God who incessantly pursued His people. David understood this love; it is evident through many of the Psalms. God was known for His mercy; He was known for His love; He was known for being selfless toward undeserving people.

I would be remiss if, when talking about the selfless nature of God, I don't speak of Christ and all He was sent to accomplish.

> For God so loved the world that he gave his one and only Son, that whoever believes in him shall not perish but have eternal life (John 3:16).

God does not have to put up with our foolish sinning, and we all sin. Yet God has created for us salvation. Do not think for one moment that He had to. There is nothing so good about you or me that forced God's arm to save us. Do you know why there was a plan set in motion within the very construct of the cosmos before the foundations of the world even were formed? The selfless nature of the Almighty God.

Scripture Index

CREDITS

Select Scriptures quotations are taken from the Holy Bible, New International Version®, NIV®. Copyright © 1973, 1978, 1984, 2011 by Biblica, Inc.™ Used by permission of Zondervan. All rights reserved worldwide. www.zondervan.com The "NIV" and "New International Version" are trademarks registered in the United States Patent and Trademark Office by Biblica, Inc.®

Select Scripture quotations are taken from the NEW KING JAMES VERSION®. Copyright© 1982 by Thomas Nelson, Inc. Used by permission. All rights reserved.

ABOUT THE AUTHOR

My name is Brian Poe and I am married to Jesse Poe. I have two boys; Caleb is just about to turn nine, and Benjamin is about to turn seven. I first began preaching for the Bad Axe Church of Christ in 2014. In late 2015, I moved back to the city where I started preaching for the Northeast Church of Christ. My final years of preaching were at the Dexter Church of Christ where I preached from 2018 to 2021. During this time, I also was pursuing my Master of Divinity through Heritage Christian University. I obtained my MDiv in 2020 and soon later began my degree in Family Therapy through Amridge University. In 2021, I shifted my ministry focus and was accepted into a chaplain residency program at Covenant Healthcare. I recently finished my residency and plan to continue my ministry as a chaplain. I have loved to write and was able to publish my first book early in 2021. My goal from here is to continue to write as I minister as a chaplain.

ALSO BY CYPRESS PUBLICATIONS

Always Near: Listening for Lessons from God
by Bill Bagents

The Christian Life: Chapters for Bible Teacher
by Ed Gallagher

Cruciform Christ: 52 Reflections on the Gospel of Mark
by Travis Bookout

Easing Life's Hurts 2nd ed.
by Jack Wilhelm and Bill Bagents

Equipping the Saints: A Practical Study of Ephesians 4:11–16
by Bill Bagents and Cory Collins

The Holy Spirit: A Bible Study Guide
by Jack Wilhelm

Jesus the Christ: Chapters for Bible Teachers
by Ed Gallagher

King of Glory: 52 Reflections on the Gospel of John
by Travis Bookout

Rescue: God and Sin in the Old Testament
by John F. Wakefield

Revisiting Life's Oases: Soul-Soothing Stories
by Bill Bagents

Welcoming God's Word: Reading with Head and Heart
by Bill Bagents

WHAM! Facing Life's Heavy Hits: Thirteen Old Testament Encounters
by Bill and Laura S. Bagents

WHAM! Facing Life's Heavy Hits: Thirteen New Testament Encounters
by Bill and Laura S. Bagents

Women in the Shadows
by Betty Hamblen

CYPRESS

To see full catalog of Heritage Christian University Press and
its imprint Cypress Publications, visit
www.hcu.edu/publications

www.ingramcontent.com/pod-product-compliance
Lightning Source LLC
Chambersburg PA
CBHW071003120626
46546CB00003B/913